THE
VIRTUAL
GUITARIST

THE VIRTUAL GUITARIST

Hardware, Software, and Websites for the Guitar

FREDERICK NOAD

SCHIRMER BOOKS
An Imprint of Simon & Schuster Macmillan
NEW YORK

Prentice Hall International
LONDON   MEXICO CITY   NEW DELHI   SINGAPORE   SYDNEY   TORONTO

Schirmer Books
An Imprint of Simon & Schuster Macmillan
1633 Broadway
New York, New York 10019

Library of Congress Catalog Card Number: 97-29047

Printed in the United States of America

Printing Number
1 2 3 4 5 6 7 8 9 10

Library of Congress Cataloging-in-Publication Data

Noad, Frederick M.
    The virtual guitarist : hardware, software, and Websites for the
    guitar / Frederick Noad.
        p. cm.
Includes index.
ISBN 0-02-864584-7 (alk. paper)
    1. Guitar—Computer programs. 2. Guitar—Computer network
resources. 3. Music—Computer programs. 4. Music—Computer network
resources. 5. Computer sound processing. I. Title
ML1015.G9N58 1998
787.87'0285—dc21   97-29047
                                                                CIP
                                                                MN

This paper meets the requirements of ANSI/NISO Z.39.48-1992 (Permanence of Paper).

We also have sound-houses, where we practise and demonstrate all sounds and their generation. . . . We represent small sounds as great and deep; likewise great sounds, extenuate and sharp; we make divers tremblings and warblings of sounds and letters, and the voices and notes of beasts and birds.
Francis Bacon, *New Atlantis* (1627)

There really wasn't a lot this machine could do that you couldn't do yourself in half the time with a lot less trouble.
Douglas Adams, *Dirk Gently's Holistic Detective Agency* (1987)*

CONTENTS

CONTENTS

Contents

CONTENTS

PREFACE

In little more than a decade the personal computer has thrust itself upon the musical scene, and the extent and sophistication of its applications multiply almost daily. Computers can create and record traditional or totally new sounds, edit and filter those sounds, write them out in traditional notation, generate orchestral parts at lightning speed, and provide vast and easily accessible storage. In addition, computers can communicate around the world through the Internet at great speed and minimal cost, providing access to huge amounts of material.

To the individual musician such wealth can at first sight seem overwhelming. The initial equipment may seem alarmingly expensive, and it may be capable of far more than is really needed. In addition, musicians may have some prejudices about the aesthetics of synthesized sound and a measure of technophobia at the sight of screens filled with dials, slider controls, wave patterns, and so on. Somewhere amid all this lie sanity and a useful tool or tools, but uninformed seekers, if they complete the search at all, are liable to waste huge amounts of time before finding what will really enhance their creative output.

For all these reasons, the present book, rather than catalog the huge volume of available materials, focuses on equipment and programs that are exceptionally easy and useful. Because the material is chosen selectively, there is room for hands-on guidance, giving the reader a specific rather than theoretical guide to buying and using both hardware and software. Also, because so much of the available software is oriented to the needs of keyboard players, this book offers specific assistance to the guitarist and string player.

For some, perhaps many, the computer may not prove to be vital to their musical advancement; the discovery of this fact here can save hours of frustration. For others, the new tools may enable them to reach their particular goals; my hope is that this book will make their connection to those tools as rapid and uncomplicated as possible.

ACKNOWLEDGMENTS

I should like to thank the manufacturers of the software discussed in this book for generously supplying review copies; Keri Walker and Doedie Hunter of Apple Computer for arranging the generous loan of equipment for this project; David Battino, editor of *Music & Computers*, for useful information and issues of the magazine; Dennis O'Neill for permission to use his original Music Notation Programs compilation as a basis for the appendix; Stephen Dick for assistance updating this list; Chris Newell for patient demonstrations of MIDISCAN; Casey Muller for computer installations and technical assistance; Don Carnes for the generous supply and maintenance of additional equipment; and finally my wife, Marilyn, for general support and practical help organizing the graphics.

TRADEMARKS

Most of the products described in this book are identified by their trade names, which are claimed as legally protected trademarks by the companies that make the products.

INTRODUCTION

I have been exploring computers since about 1983, when I bought my first machine, a Commodore 64. Absolutely delighted with it, I used it for word processing and to learn some fundamentals of programming using the LOGO language. I wanted to develop an easy-to-use music typewriter, and this spurred my overall interest. With the simplicity of plugging a small cartridge into the back I was able to play Pac Man, and its telltale tones and squeaks gave me away many times when I should have been working.

Next came the Atari ST, a wonderful machine that also would support my LOGO programming experiments. With this I wrote a simple scoring program, and also one to convert guitar or lute tablature to conventional notation. More sophisticated games were available, but somehow they never had the magic appeal of the first Pac Man games. I would probably still be using the Atari were it not for the emergence of the Macintosh, which I resisted at first as being too expensive and inconvenient in not communicating with the printers that I already owned. On the Atari my scoring program had progressed to the C language—a more professional form of coding—and I was able to use it for my classes and arranging. The Macintosh became the more popular machine, however, and was by now the acknowledged leader in the area of desktop publishing owing to its superior handling of fonts, PostScript printing, and so on.

The next stage for me was to bow out from programming, which I yielded to two brilliant computer science majors in their final year of study, Chris Conway and Todd Stewart. Chris laid down the architecture for what was to become SpeedScore (a scoring program described in chapter 3), and Todd worked with him, adding much innovation in the area of automatic beaming and curve drawing. I was more or less relegated to font production and testing, both of which involved a totally unexpected amount of work. Other programmers have added their expertise, and now SpeedScore is on the market. What started as a hobby grew in its demands, although the goal was the same as the original one on the Commodore 64—to produce a very easy-to-use music typewriter.

I relate this saga mainly to explain how a classical guitarist could become so enmeshed in the world of computers, and also to explain the background for feeling bold enough to present a book like this. I have had the opportunity to "look under the hood" of computers and programming, and as a result to look at many music programs.

While this book is directed mainly at classical guitarists like myself, I hope the information will be found useful by many other players of bowed, blown, or plucked instruments. These musicians tend to be left behind in the forward march of keyboard-oriented computer programs.

For many of these programs the goal is to make complex, polyphonic arrangements and compositions achievable by a single technophile composer, whose principal input tool is a pianolike keyboard. Film and television sound tracks abound with music of this kind, some of which is eventually converted to scores for performance by a live orchestra. Sadly, much more is not, and the final, computer-generated sound track represents lost opportunities for studio musicians. Gone are the days when the violinists driving into the parking lot of Local 47, Hollywood, could be identified by their new Cadillacs. The equivalent high earners today are more likely to be computer-savvy pop composers with a well-equipped home studio.

To the average student, teacher, and even professional player of non-keyboard instruments, these programs may seem impossibly high tech. Nevertheless, programs do exist with simpler purposes, and some of these may be found useful and even valuable. For instance, the most useful programs for the instrumental teacher are probably those that will produce a good-looking score in advance of the arrival of a student or class. Such music can be stored in the computer and printed out at will, and using the right program can be much preferable to hauling out an ink pen to make a fair copy, particularly because of the ease of correcting mistakes with the computer. More than anything else, this ability to fix mistakes easily, coupled with the ability to cut and paste without large-scale retyping, is what drew writers away from their favorite typewriter to the computer keyboard. And what is true of word processors is generally true of music scoring programs, several of which are discussed in chapter 3.

Moreover, the computer can now be used as an audio recording machine; several ways to do this are discussed in chapter 4, along with the overall pros and cons. Closer seemingly to magic is the world of optical character recognition for music, where a computer examines an existing piece of sheet music that has been optically scanned and produces from it an audible playback or perhaps an enhanced and cleaned-up score. Two such systems are examined in detail in chapter 5.

Computers can also be used as a teaching aid to assist in the understanding of harmony, counterpoint, scale construction, ear training, and more. A particularly well thought-out example of this, Practica Musica by Jeffrey Evans, is explored in chapter 6. The CD-ROM, with its ability to store and play both audio and video material and to present this material interactively is another fertile source for music education and exploration. Some of the better examples from this rather sparse area are also visited in chapter 6.

Inevitably today the Internet must loom large in any discussion of computer resources. The speed of growth in this area is so phenomenal that it is impossible to deplore the dearth of resources on any given topic today, since those resources may be there tomorrow. Some of what exists today is explored in chapters 7–12, together with the basics of connection and operation.

To make a start, the basics of computers and computer music are discussed in the first two chapters. I hope to demystify some of the jargon and to show how useful the computer can be for guitarists and other musicians. The computer is an extraordinarily versatile tool, but like all tools, it is worthless until one knows how to use it. It is my hope that this book will increase the working knowledge not only of computer novices but also of guitarists who have already discovered how much the computer can aid them in their musical lives.

ONE
COMPUTER
BASICS

A STARTING POINT

This book is written as an introduction to the use of computers; no prior knowledge is assumed. It is much easier to skip ahead if you already know something than to struggle with unexplained concepts and terminology, so if this section is too basic for you, just move along to the appropriate starting point for your level of expertise. If, on the other hand, you have resisted computers for fear that they are too complex to learn, read on at least to find that the basics are simple and understandable. The complexity comes with individual programs, and just as a piano can sound simple or miraculously sophisticated according to the player, so computers can seem amazing when taught new tricks by a skillful programmer.

COMPUTERS ARE ESSENTIALLY SIMPLE

Computers deal in numbers and have no intelligence. They can *seem* intelligent when we make the numbers stand for something, as when each letter in the alphabet is assigned a number so we can make sentences and blocks of text. But the text we type in and store resides in the computer as a series of numbers and nothing else.

The way we store the numbers is again simple. Memory cells are switched either on or off, representing a 1 or a 0. Any number can be expressed this way, and where we would count 1, 2, 3, 4, and so on, the computer counts 1, 10, 11, 100, since it has only the two numeric possibilities. This is known as a *binary* system. Obviously this makes for some rather long sets of ones and zeros, but computers have plenty of space for these. The numbers find their way to temporary storage, known as *random-access memory* (RAM), or to a more permanent place on a storage

1

disk. Small-capacity disks are known as *floppy disks*, although most are not floppy anymore, and these can be inserted into and removed from the computer's floppy disk drive, which is used to read the disk contents into the computer. In contrast, the computer's *hard disk*, which normally resides inside the case of the computer, has much more memory capacity. The capacity is not unlimited, however, and old unwanted material must normally be eliminated to make place for new items.

A final category of memory is *read-only memory* (ROM), which cannot be altered by the operator and is used internally by the computer, usually as part of its operating system. The term is also used in connection with the now familiar *CD-ROM*, which stores very large amounts of data on a compact laser disk, and which can feed information into the computer through an appropriate drive in a way similar to the floppy disk but with about six hundred times as much storage. Here the term *ROM* is used because the user can only read from a CD-ROM and not write data to it.

The computer's purpose and existence depend on *programs*, which are often supplied on floppy disks and transferred onto the computer's hard drive for long-term use. Programs are generically known as *software* because they traditionally resided on floppy disks rather than being built into the computer's hardware. Like an electric drill, which can be transformed into a grinder or polisher according to what accessory is installed, the computer becomes a tool for drawing pictures or composing music according to the ingenuity of the program used.

WHY USE A COMPUTER AT ALL?

One of the main issues addressed by this book is the question of whether one needs to use a computer at all. Perhaps the best start is to look at how the computer has been used successfully by millions of people in other fields. Probably the most familiar application is word processing. Almost all professional writers have turned from handwriting, typing, or even dictating to using computers. The reason: typing corrections can be made with great ease, sentences and whole paragraphs can be cut and pasted from one place to another, and the whole document can easily be checked for spelling errors. Many writers held out for years because they liked the feel of a favorite pen, or because they assumed that their thinking process would in some way be mechanized and corrupted. But the holdouts are very few now. I began this book thinking I would prefer to work with a large bound volume of blank pages, writing with a pen and drawing in graphics and music as I went along. In fact, though, I yielded to the convenience of the computer. The bound book is wonderful for quick access, but the computer is so much better when it comes to correcting, rearranging, and finalizing. Also, I can easily copy in the graphics as I go along.

The musical parallel to the word processor is the scoring program, which substitutes the computer for the laborious hand copying of music. Although the entry of music into a computer is not without labor, the resulting clean, legible printed page is sufficient incentive for many. (Music scoring programs are dealt with in detail in chapter 3.)

Next comes the proofreading stage, which for an author simply means invoking the word processor's built-in spelling checker. Music is harder to check, as any publisher will agree, and it is also a fact that the ear is better than the eye for many types of mistake. For instance, a missing sharp or flat can easily escape a visual check, but the sound of the resulting wrong note makes the error stand out. For this reason many scoring programs include the ability to play back the written music that has been entered.

At least one music program now is capable of *optical character recognition*, or OCR. Such a program scans a piece of printed music, recognizes the musical symbols, and converts the notes into a computer file that may then be used to make a playback sequence. Once the music is heard, the program user may choose to edit the piece or produce a better-looking score than the original. OCR is dealt with in chapter 5. For now let's consider the question of choosing hardware.

WHICH COMPUTER SHOULD I BUY?

A few years ago the decision over which computer to buy was more difficult because there were several options. Now the majority of software manufacturers have decided to develop programs for only two computer types (sometimes known as *platforms*), the Apple Macintosh and the IBM PC. The term *PC* (for *personal computer*) usually refers to the IBM and its emulators, but newer Macintosh models are known as Power PCs, a name that tends to confuse the issue. In fact, present-day users hope that the two types will grow closer and in a few years be indistinguishable, but for now a choice has to made.

APPLE OR IBM?

From the user's standpoint, the main difference between Apple and IBM computers is in the look and feel of each platform's *operating system*, the "background" software that controls the machine's basic functions, as opposed to software for specific applications, such as word processing, accounting, mechanical drawing, and so on. Again, the gap between the two platforms has been narrowing in recent years in this regard, but for most people a preference for one operating system or the other remains, along with price, a major deciding factor in choosing a computer.

In the early 1980s Apple acquired from Xerox Corporation an operating system that opened a new era for computer users. The system used small on-screen pictures, or *icons*, to identify programs, data files, and so on. These icons were the brainchild of Alan Kay, a brilliant young member of the Xerox PARC, a research group that also developed the *mouse*— essentially a movable switch used to move a pointer around the screen for the purpose of selecting visible items. Usually this involved clicking a button on the mouse when the pointer had been maneuvered to the required item. Items could also be moved to different places on the screen by holding down the button and dragging the mouse around on the worktable. The system worked so well that it has now become the standard on both platforms.

Until recent years at least, the Apple Macintosh, introduced in 1983, has been the easier system to set up and use, owing to the company's "plug and play" policy. Under this policy a piece of equipment only needs to be plugged into the power supply and to its associated units to be fully operative. Unfortunately, this has not always been the case with IBM-compatible equipment, whose operating system, DOS, requires the user to type in *commands*, strings of letters and numbers that the nonspecialist generally finds arcane and hard to remember. That difficulty was largely overcome with the introduction of Windows, a graphic interface that lets the operator use a mouse to point and click at icons, much like the Apple operating system. Windows 95, the latest version, comes even closer to erasing the distinctions between the look and feel of Apple and IBM computers.

A further deciding factor, of course, is price. Because IBM did not keep a tight proprietary hold on its technology, rival manufacturers of IBM "clones" sprang up like mushrooms. The resulting proliferation of equipment and highly competitive pricing made PCs generally cheaper than Macs. However, the recent appearance of Macintosh "clones" made under license by other manufacturers promises to change that picture.

Another result of the IBM price wars is that there are today many more PCs than Macintoshes. This of course tends to make the software manufacturers favor the PC simply because the sales potential is larger. Consequently, many computer buyers, especially in the business world, tend to go for IBM machines because they want specific software that is available only for DOS or Windows platforms. However, in the areas of graphics, desktop publishing, and to a large extent music, designers have continued to create programs for the Macintosh, whose more "intuitive" operating system gained it an early foothold among artists and musicians. The descriptions of music software in the chapters that follow specify whether a program is available for the Mac, PC, or both. Computers may be augmented by extra pieces of hardware, known generically as *peripherals*. For instance, a *scanner*, which looks like a small copying machine, enables pictures and printed text to be entered into the computer. Once entered, pictures may be edited with graphics programs, and text may be processed just as if it had been typed in. In addition, musical symbols can be scanned in from sheet music for various purposes discussed in chapter 5. Another important peripheral is the *modem*, used for communication over phone lines to send faxes or connect with the Internet and other services. For the musician there are *sound cards,* plug-in devices that can generate musical sounds and speech and provide the means for recording and playback. The Macintosh has musical capability built into its logic board, but the PC, without the addition of a sound card, is limited to a warning beep. Sound cards are discussed in more detail in chapter 2.

This book has been written with a Power Macintosh 7600, which I've also used to test all Macintosh music programs and CD-ROMs. The PC programs have been tested in a Windows environment.

SOME BASIC COMPUTER TERMS

Throughout this book it is necessary to use some common computer terms. If you know them already, skip this section and continue to chapter 2. If you don't know the terms, you will find the descriptions helpful even if you don't yet have a computer, since they will be immediately useful to you when you finally make a start.

THE KEYBOARD

Until the Macintosh computer burst onto the scene in the early 1980s, most instructions to the computer were entered from the computer's keyboard, which closely resembles a traditional typewriter keyboard with the addition of a numeric keypad in adding machine format and a few additional keys.

THE MOUSE

Keyboards are still important, but the computer mouse has become ever more popular, since it is usually faster to make a mouse choice than to type a command in words. The mouse fits comfortably in the palm of the hand, and when it is in position the index finger can press down on a switch, a process known as *clicking the mouse.* As the mouse is moved around by the hand on the tabletop or on a pad made for the purpose, a pointer moves around the computer screen. The standard pointer is usually a small arrow, but the shape may change for special purposes.

The most common use of the mouse is to make selections from the screen by clicking on options presented by the computer in graphic form. Here is a typical example: I have done some typing in a word processing program, and I attempt to close the program without taking the necessary steps to save my work. Fortunately, a message appears on the screen in a *dialog box,* which gives me the chance to interact with the computer by selecting one of the three options. I can now make my choice by clicking the mouse in the appropriate box. This type of dialog box is also known as an *alert box* because it alerts you to something that needs to be done.

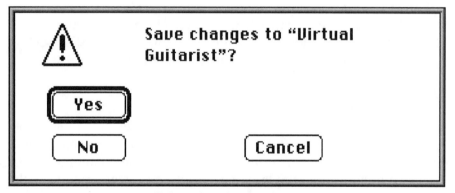

A dialog (alert) box on the Mac

The other common use of the mouse is to make choices from *menus.* These lists of choices are usually positioned at the top of the screen and drop down when the mouse is moved into the area. For instance, here I have moved my mouse pointer over the word "Font" and pressed the mouse down.

The font choices appear and, still holding down the button, I move the mouse pointer down to make my selection. When I arrive at my choice, here Courier, I release the button. In response, the computer puts a check mark beside the item to show me my choice has been successfully made and turns the lettering into white on black for additional clarity. This is often referred to as *reverse video.*

Using the mouse this way with the button held down is known as a *click/drag* operation. It is often used to move icons and other visual elements around the screen. For instance, if you were to click the mouse on the icon shown below, holding the button down after pressing the switch,

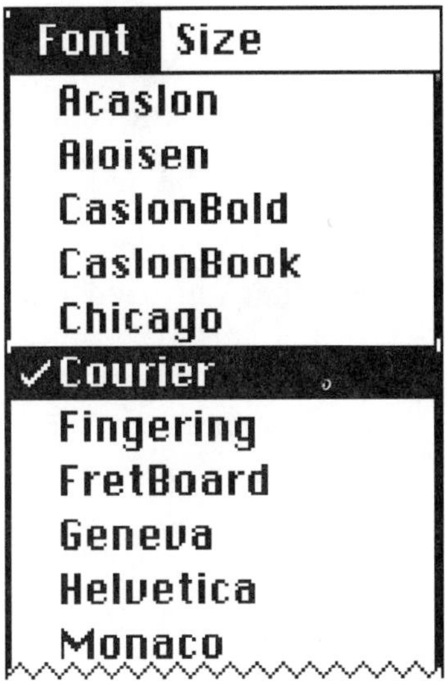

Font	Size
Acaslon	
Aloisen	
CaslonBold	
CaslonBook	
Chicago	
✓**Courier**	
Fingering	
FretBoard	
Geneva	
Helvetica	
Monaco	

A drop-down menu

you could drag the icon to a new position. To release it you simply let go of the button.

Another common use of the mouse is the *double click*—two quick clicks of the mouse, one after the other. This is commonly used to start programs running, the double click being made on either a text or pictorial identification of the program. Various terms are used for starting a pro-

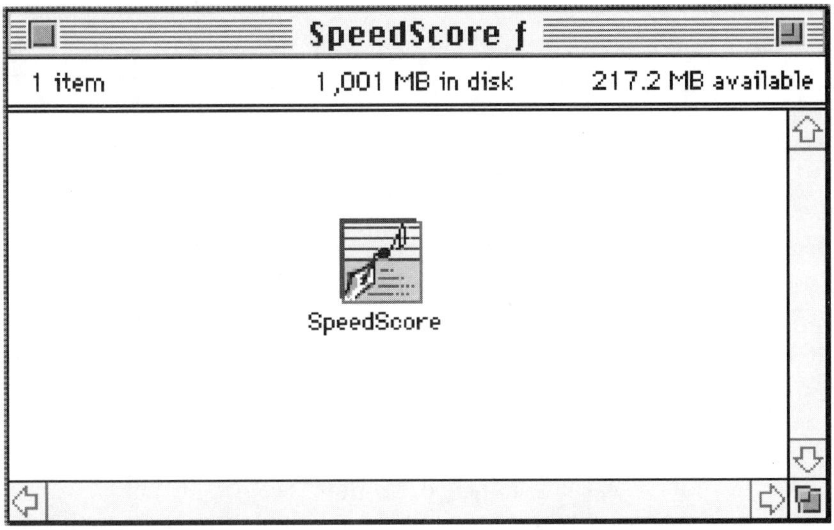

SpeedScore ƒ		
1 item	1,001 MB in disk	217.2 MB available

SpeedScore

Click/drag to move the icon around; double click to start the program

7

gram, including *executing, launching,* and *running,* with no difference in meaning.

The basic screen that appears after starting up the Macintosh or Windows is often referred to as the *desktop,* being the starting point for all work operations.

The above is by no means a comprehensive computer tutorial. Rather, it simply defines a few terms that are used frequently throughout this book.

TWO
COMPUTER SOUND GENERATION: THE BASICS

The types of sound generated by a computer can be simply divided into two categories: artificial sounds created by electronic synthesis, and reproductions of actual instruments or voices. Individual notes can be recorded once and stored for later access, a process known as *sampling;* or the computer can simply be used for recording and playback, much like a conventional tape recorder. Although sampled sound can have a high quality compared to that produced by electronic sound generators, it rarely sounds completely like the original instrument owing, for instance, to the lack of the subtle and varying sounds of lip, bow, or fingernail in the initial attack. Also, for reasons of compactness only certain notes are sampled, and these are changed in pitch to supply the full range, resulting in less convincing simulations. Sampling seems more successful in simulating instruments that are mechanical in the first place, such as harpsichords or organs.

The first synthesizers appeared in the 1960s, the best known being probably those of Robert Moog. In 1968 the highly successful record *Switched-On Bach,* which was performed on a Moog synthesizer, brought the terminology and the concept to a much wider public.

MODERN SYNTHESIZERS

Synthesizer manufacturers have followed widely different methods of creating sounds, with results that must be judged by personal preference rather than by any arbitrary standard. Originally, popular interest in the synthesizer focused on its somewhat limited ability to imitate other instruments. Perhaps the closest parallel historically is the pipe organ, whose stops rarely sounded much like the instruments they supposedly imitated. Ultimately great organs were judged for their own magnificence rather than the accuracy of their stops, and today synthesizers are valued as much for their originality as for their ability to imitate.

Electronic keyboards often contain a built-in synthesizer, particularly the inexpensive ones designed for the mass market. In contrast, high-end keyboards usually produce no sound of their own, but are used to play the musician's choice of stand-alone synthesizers, black boxes often called *modules.* Such keyboards belong to the family of devices known as *controllers,* since their function is not to produce sound but to control something that does. The best controllers have weighted keys that are sensitive to the player's touch and attack. Controllers can also be built to resemble other instruments, such as the guitar and the saxophone; regardless of appearance, they all are essentially transmitters of information that physically simulate musical instruments for the convenience of the player.

Although synthesizer quality is a matter of personal taste, it is safe to say that an expensive synthesizer developed by a major company in the field will produce sounds of more complexity and appeal than those included with inexpensive electronic keyboards. All synthesizers will include at least one simulated guitar sound, although a convincing classical guitar sound is still hard to find. This is a case where "try before you buy" is particularly important.

SOUND CARDS

For everyday use a synthesizer that fits inside a computer as a plug-in device can substitute for an external black box. Such internal synthesizers, or *sound cards,* frequently contain the necessary circuitry to play audio CD recordings. In addition to playing both audio and digital tracks, these masterpieces of miniaturization usually include an audio amplifier with output to speakers as well as a line connection to link up with a larger amplifier such as the home stereo system. Sound cards are necessary for playing the audio tracks of a CD-ROM, so if you buy a computer that already contains a CD-ROM drive chances are that it will contain a sound card as well as the other CD-ROM necessities. In addition it may well include a microphone or line input, which enables you to record audio with your computer, and a MIDI input/output plug (see below). Musically speaking, direct-to-disk recording can achieve very high quality. The sound received by the microphone is converted into digital form and stored on the computer's hard drive. The digital system used is essentially the same as that for commercial CDs, and in this case the computer becomes a substitute for a tape recorder. However, music recorded this way consumes huge amounts of disk storage space. In contrast, synthesized (MIDI) sound is normally stored very compactly in the form of a series of instructions. These instructions, which are really a sequence of switching operations, are known as MIDI tracks, and these tracks can be played by an internal synthesizer or sent to several different synthesizers at the same time. In addition, live recorded sound can be mixed with synthesizer-generated tracks to produce the effect of multi-instrument ensembles. Obviously, this kind of production is not for everyone, but because the basic equipment is now readily available at a comparatively moderate price, this subject is discussed at some length in chapter 4.

WHAT IS MIDI?

As mentioned above, MIDI is essentially a switching code. The rather grand name Musical Instrument Digital Interface is misleading, since the code has nothing to do with actual musical instruments and could in fact be used to control a system of garden sprinkers, a light show for a rock concert, or the billboards in Times Square. It is most commonly used for music, however, and the sound generators that it controls can be considered as instruments.

The MIDI standard, or *protocol,* was developed to simplify the interaction between devices from different manufacturers, and it has been widely supported by the industry. MIDI is most easily conceived by considering a child's toy piano that has only eight notes, corresponding to a C major scale. Suppose that each note has a number from one to eight written on it, starting at the lowest, and you tell the child to play the appropriate note as you call out a number. When you call out "One one five five six six five," and if the child responds correctly, you will hear the melody of "Twinkle, Twinkle, Little Star." What you called out was a *sequence,* comparable to a MIDI sequence, which resulted in musical notes being produced. You could have used the same sequence to cue another child with an appropriately numbered xylophone, or you could have had them both play at once. In essence, a MIDI sequence is simply a series of numbers that produce an agreed-upon response. Extending from that simple note instruction, you would want to refine your sequence to be able to signal which notes are to last longer, which are louder or softer, and so on. As well as variations in pitch, volume, and duration the current MIDI standard supports such subtleties as pitch bend and vibrato.

MIDI OUT/IN/THROUGH

When a MIDI sequence is sent to a MIDI instrument such as a synthesizer, it goes from a MIDI OUT connection on the controller (usually a pianolike keyboard) to the synthesizer's MIDI IN socket via a standard MIDI cable. In addition, you can send the controller output to a computer (data then go from the controller's MIDI OUT to the computer's MIDI IN). The computer can store this information and act as a type of recording machine. What is actually recorded is the series of control numbers, and since storing numbers is very economical of computer disk space, huge amounts of MIDI information can be stored in a small space. To play the stored information as music, the file is sent either to an internal sound card or, via a MIDI OUT plug, to an external synthesizer. Sometimes the MIDI information is required to go to two or more synthesizers. Rather than have separate cables from the controller to each synthesizer, the MIDI information can be taken from synthesizer no. 1 to no. 2 via a MIDI THROUGH output on no. 1 to the MIDI IN input on no. 2. In simple terms, the MIDI flow of numbers goes in one direction only through a standard MIDI cable.

ANALOG AND DIGITAL RECORDING

Before the digital era, music was recorded by converting sound waves into a form analogous to them in frequency and magnitude, hence referred to as *analog recording.* Here is an example of a pure sound expressed graphically. The height of the wave represents the volume, and the width the frequency.

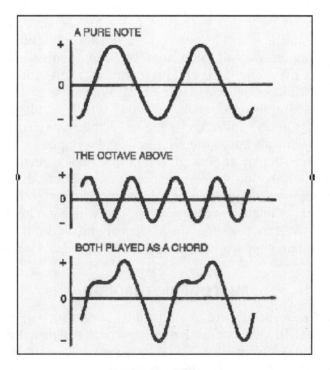

Analog sound waves

These sound waves could be stored in a number of ways, the earliest including the cutting of a track on a revolving cylinder and later a disk. A needle traveling in the groove would vibrate with similar loudness and pitch, and mechanical devices, such as large horns, amplified the needle's vibrations to make the result audible. Later it was found that the vibrations could be amplified electrically, and that a measure of tone control could be added to increase fidelity. The electrical vibrations could be stored on magnetic wire or tape, making editing much easier, and the edited version could be used to make master disks that could be duplicated in vinyl. The vibrating needle in the vinyl produced a varying electrical signal through the phonograph pickup, and this was again amplified and tonally corrected (or *equalized*) on its way to playback through a loudspeaker.

Digital recording, in contrast, involves converting the sound waves into a series of numbers that can be easily handled by a computer. This is done by taking a series of measurements of the characteristics of a sound wave, storing these measurements sequentially, and later reconstructing the wave from these measurements. The measurements are numbers, which can be stored in digital form as 1s and 0s. So now, like a MIDI sequence, the necessary information has become nothing but a series of numbers.

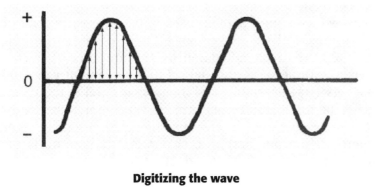

Digitizing the wave

Here the parallel with MIDI ends, however, since an accurate representation of a waveform takes a huge quantity of numbers. For typical commercial CD production the sound wave is measured over forty-one thousand times per second, and each measurement results in a number. This huge store of numbers represents enough information to reconstruct the wave at a later point with considerable fidelity.

STORING THE RECORDINGS

Since the economy of storage space associated with MIDI files does not, unfortunately, apply to direct-to-disk recording, the computer used must have a very large amount of memory available for storage. One minute of stereo music recording will require some ten megabytes of storage space, and if editing is to take place, at least another ten. As an alternative, a tape recorder is more commonly used for recording, the digital variety being known as DAT recorders. A DAT tape is much less expensive than a computer disk for storage, by a factor of at least one to twenty, so the choice of which to use will depend on the amount and type of editing required. When the information is in the computer it is easy to edit in sophisticated ways. For further details see chapter 4.

Before discussing examples of actual equipment and software in the chapters to come, the following points may provide an overview.

1. **Scoring programs.** For the general musician, scoring programs may be among the most useful computer aids, since they do for the musician what a word processor does for an author. They vary considerably in additional features, which may include MIDI sequencing.

2. **MIDI devices** are widely used for recording synthesized musical sounds for radio and TV commercials and for the background music of films. They can imitate drums and other forms of percussion very convincingly, and can be used to create totally original sounds for contemporary scores and effects.

3. **Synthesized sound** is often used to back up voices or true instruments for commercial recordings, since the artificiality of an all-synthesized ensemble is much alleviated by the presence of even a single human voice. A lone performer with MIDI equipment can produce the effect of a very large ensemble, and if he has the ability to mix true audio tracks with the MIDI, the results can be very impressive. The classical guitarist may be interested in creating simulated ensemble or orchestral backgrounds for practice purposes. Otherwise, he is unlikely to become much involved in this type of sound, since it lacks the essential subtlety of an acoustic instrument.

4. **Digital recording** is here to stay for one big reason. Digital recordings, like MIDI sequences, can be duplicated with virtually no loss because only numbers are being copied. As a result, a copy made from a copy of an original (known technically as a *second-generation* copy) can be as perfect as the original. With conventional tape recording each successive generation introduces loss or unwanted noise. In addition, digital recordings can be edited in a computer in sophisticated ways, and when the recording is stored on the computer's hard drive, different areas can be quickly accessed without waiting for tape to wind back or forward.

14

One of the most useful editing features is that an alteration may be heard and approved before it is finally made. For the guitar soloist this obviously has tremendous appeal, since an unwanted finger click or other noise can be skillfully trimmed out of a recording.

COMMON RECORDING TERMS

Newcomers to these topics might wish to consider the following commonly used terms.

Analog recording. An analogy or representation of a sound wave is captured for later playback. Volume, pitch, and so on remain in wave form.

A to D. An abbreviation for "analog to digital," for instance, when the electrical wave from a microphone is converted to digital form.

D to A. The reverse process, as for instance when digital information is converted by a CD player to play through a loudspeaker.

DAT recorder. A tape recorder used for digital recording.

Digital recording. The incoming wave form is converted to binary numbers for storage. For playback the numbers can be used to reconstruct a wave.

MIDI controller. The device that sends the MIDI sequence, usually a piano-type keyboard or MIDI guitar.

MIDI sequence. A file containing a sequence of MIDI instructions.

MIDI sequencer. The computer program that enables a MIDI sequence to be constructed. Data may be entered by computer keyboard or by a MIDI instrument.

Sampler. A device used to make digital samples of a waveform for storage and later playback. Often used to sample actual musical instruments for storage within a synthesizer.

Scoring program. A program to write and print musical scores.

Synthesizer. A sound generator that imitates musical or original sounds.

THREE
SCORING PROGRAMS

Scoring programs vary from those dedicated to producing publishable music, perhaps best considered as engraving programs, to those that produce simple scores that, while usable in informal surroundings, lack the finish and accuracy necessary for publication. The latter type are usually found as an adjunct to MIDI sequencing programs, showing in score form music that has been entered from a MIDI keyboard or guitar. Such scores can usually be edited and printed, but are not really intended for publication or professional studio use. Often the editing capabilities are awkward, and such features as fingering or dynamic signs are unavailable. Nonetheless, they serve a purpose for the newcomer to music notation, since they will create a score that is at least readable from an improvised performance.

PIANO KEYBOARD ENTRY

By playing the music to be scored on the piano-type keyboard in rhythm, the musician can enter both pitches and note values in one operation. Because the computer tends to be more accurate in rhythm than the player, however, the program's transcription of the rhythm may at first seem strange ("Did I really play it like that?"). For example, here is what I *thought* I played in with a MIDI keyboard:

MIDI keyboard entry: What was intended

And here is how it was transcribed by a top-rated MIDI sequencer (Opcode's Studio Vision):

MIDI keyboard entry: What the computer heard

Obviously, the program attempted to notate fine rhythmic subtleties that I had no intention of making. Fortunately, there are ways to make the computer ignore very small time variations that are likely to be unintended. This process is known as *quantizing*. After the Quantize feature was set to ignore anything less than an eighth note, things improved.

MIDI Keyboard entry: After quantizing

Still, the computer was much more accurate than I was, and considerable editing was necessary to straighten things out. For me it was much quicker to enter the notes directly from the computer keyboard into an engraving program, in this case SpeedScore. Nevertheless, skill can be acquired in playing with extreme accuracy, and for some this will an acceptable form of entry.

Guitarists will wonder at this point whether a MIDI guitar can be used for note entry. In fact it can; this is perhaps the only really satisfactory use of that instrument. The topic was well summed up by Joseph Thompson in an Internet discussion:

> I am sure some systems are better that others, but if a player's reason for getting a MIDI guitar setup is to play his/her classical gui-

tar repertoire while sounding like a cathedral organ or the Boston Philharmonic, I fear they will be disappointed. In general, when a MIDI system has to read and translate so much information so quickly, there are times when it isn't sure what note was played. In these cases, it is designed to make an educated guess. The guesses are usually way off the mark. Also, the system will attempt to read buzzes and squeaks as notes, which could be a major embarrassment in a performance. As far as tracking, when I am entering one note at a time or one chord at a time into Finale (almost like typing) my system is very smooth and problem free.

SOME AVAILABLE SCORING PROGRAMS

SPEEDSCORE: AN INEXPENSIVE ENGRAVING TOOL

D & H Sales
5541 Denny Avenue
N. Hollywood, California 91601

Manufacturer's Description:

"SpeedScore is a professional-level program that sets high-quality music notation for the printed page. It runs on Macintosh computers, with a Windows version expected in 1997. It offers efficient input, a high degree of control over design and styling elements, on-screen editing of musical notation, typesetting and page formatting capabilities, drawing routines, fully adjustable automatic beaming, and output to PostScript devices. TrueType fonts are also supplied. The fonts are custom designed and unique to this software. The notes may be proofed with a simple audio playback system."

It is perhaps appropriate to start with SpeedScore since it was designed by myself and is the simplest of the scoring programs discussed in this book. As the name implies, this program attempts to make the production of a finished and publishable score as simple a process as taking a pen out of a drawer and creating an ink fair copy. Even the startup time was kept to a minimum so the program could be up and running in no more time than it takes to find pen and paper. All entry of notes is done with the mouse and computer keyboard, comparable to the production of text with a word processor. There are no MIDI devices to configure or hook up, so music can be equally well entered into a laptop computer. SpeedScore comes with its own proprietary fonts, based on historic fine engraving stamps, and even includes such features as French lute tablature. For the more modern world there are chord grids for guitar or other instruments (the number of strings is variable) and drum, slash, and harmonic notes, all of which can be automatically beamed.

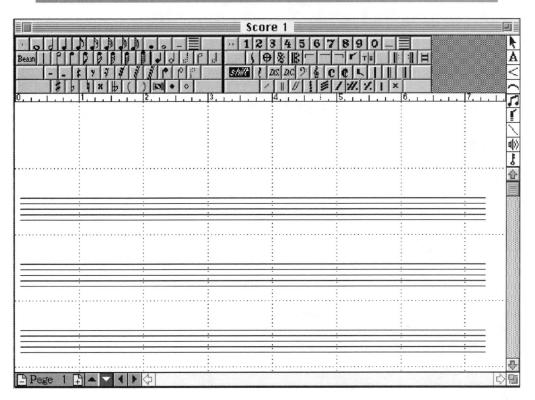

SpeedScore: The initial workscreen

I decided to enter a few measures of Tarrega's famous "Adelita," a fairly typical guitar score.

The illustration shows the working area of a SpeedScore page. At the top of the screen are a number of musical symbols arranged in the form of two keyboard sets. The one on the left represents the standard keyboard, while the one on the right represents the keys accessed when the shift key is down.

Any of these characters may be selected simply by moving the mouse cursor up to the top of the screen and clicking on the required item. This changes the mouse cursor into that item, which may be subsequently stamped onto the page anywhere by clicking again.

The setting up was simple; click on the staff character at the top of the screen and move the mouse pointer (which has now become a piece of staff) to where I want the left margin. A click, and the staff is drawn across the screen.

The characters can also be selected by pressing the appropriate key, which in the same way turns the mouse cursor into that item ready to be stamped into place. For instance, the number "1" produces a whole note, the number "2" a half note, and so on. This is the quicker method, since normally the left hand is choosing symbols and the right hand is stamping them into place, and this two-handed operation can become quite fast.

The two "keyboards" shown at the top of the SpeedScore workscreen are in fact only two out of a total of eight available. The others, accessible with a simple key choice, make available a huge palette of music, tablature, slur, and fingering symbols, including all the specialized symbols for guitar notation.

Beaming is a simple matter. The mouse is used to draw a rectangle around the notes to be beamed, and when the mouse button is released the beaming is done automatically. Beam heights or angles are easily adjusted.

SpeedScore: Beaming notes

In the first example the notes to be beamed have been enclosed by a rectangle using the mouse. When the mouse button is released, the beam appears automatically, as in the second example.

Music and tablature are entered by the same simple method. Here is an example of a workscreen using both.

The handy one-inch grid used for page layout may be switched off when not needed.

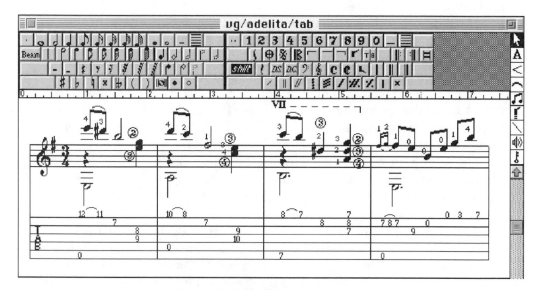

SpeedScore: "Adelita" in score and tablature

Here is how it looks when printed by the laser printer at a resolution of 300 dots per inch (dpi):

Adelita

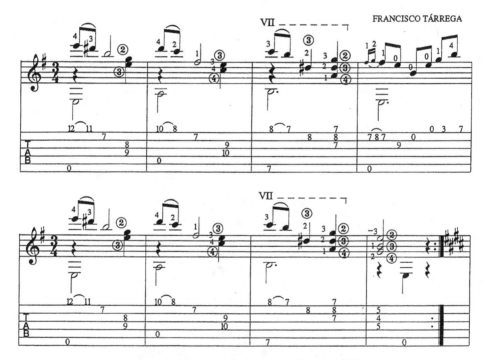

SpeedScore: "Adelita" printed at 300 dpi

Lute tablature may also be easily entered. The example here uses French tablature characters based on those used by Adrien Le Roy in the early sixteenth century.

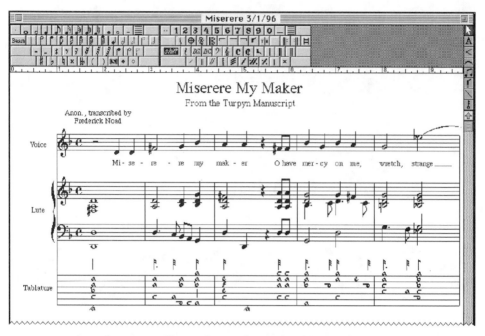

SpeedScore: Staff notation and French tablature for the lute

A miniature full page view is available at all times to check page layout.

SpeedScore: Miniature page view

Finally, a look at the printed result.

SpeedScore: The printed page

Working in Two Sizes

SpeedScore makes it possible to work in two sizes. The notes are entered at an easy-to-read size, in this case 24 and 32 points, then reduced for final printing.

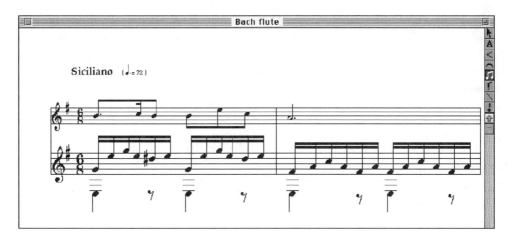

Bach Siciliano, setting in two sizes for flute and guitar

SpeedScore is designed on the analogy of the engraver's stamp, which was used originally to punch note symbols onto a soft metal plate on which the staves had been scribed with a cutting tool. The engraver needed to plan his page in advance, a process known as "casting off," by marking up the main elements of the layout with a form of shorthand code. Then, with the layout fully worked out, he or she could make the final impressions to the plate.

Nowadays the music to be engraved is usually marked up with a blue pencil to show the number of measures per line, line endings, page endings, and so on. Some computer programs will try to do this planning for you; you enter your music in a seemingly endless line, and when finished, you switch to a full-page view in which the computer has spaced your entries to fit one or more pages. It is undoubtedly convenient to have some of these functions automated, but of course in bowing to the computer's layout you concede an element of design and control. The better programs will then allow you to make adjustments until the result is to your liking. SpeedScore leaves it to you, and what you plan is what you get. Unlike the finality of the metal plate, however, on a SpeedScore working page there are many tools available to tighten up or expand the layout.

SpeedScore has text capabilities, for entering lyrics or indications of tempo and dynamics; these include choices of font, size, style, and so forth. For musicians requiring more elaborate page layout facilities, the music page may easily be imported into popular programs such as Page-Maker. SpeedScore may have multiple pages on the screen, making it easy to cut and paste parts from a multiline score. In addition, SpeedScore segments can easily be cut and pasted into most word processors, making the preparation of academic theses and similar documents easy.

The printing of music with SpeedScore is of the highest quality, since the fonts supplied with the program use the PostScript page description language. This means that the finished score can be printed from the many types of printer, from desktop laser or ink jet to photographic typesetting machines. When Linotronic prints (known colloquially as "linos") are made, the results are comparable to prints from engraved plates.

Playback in SpeedScore

A simple playback system is available for proofreading what has been entered, since the ear tends to be more accurate than the eye in this regard. Without any complicated MIDI hookups the notes can be heard, for proofreading purposes.

From the *toolbox* of icons at the top right of the workscreen a click selects the icon resembling a loudspeaker. The mouse pointer now changes to resemble this icon, which may be dragged along the musical staff. As it passes the notes these are sounded, providing an instant audible check of what has been written. This is technically known as a *scrub playback.*

SpeedScore: The playback symbol has been selected

In summary, SpeedScore is an easy-to-learn program for musicians who know what they want to see on the page. It will not make many decisions for you, but it will enable you to prepare a top-quality score to fit your concept, and to hear the notes at any point. It is currently available for the Macintosh, with a PC version expected to be released in mid-1998.

CONCERTWARE

Jump Software
201 San Antonio Circle, Suite 172
Mountain View, California 94040
Macintosh or PC

Manufacturer's Description:

"ConcertWare is an award-winning music software program that has been updated to include a Windows version and includes many new features. Students can quickly record music using the computer keyboard or any MIDI instrument. The music displays on the screen in standard notation. Students can then play back, edit, and print professional-quality sheet music. An on-screen piano keyboard functions as both a recording and playback device. Point and click on the keys and music appears on the staff. During playback, students can watch the notes flash on the keyboard in unison with the scrolling score on the staff. Includes easy-to-use 'tape deck' style buttons that allow the student to play and record easily without accessing menu commands. Documentation is completely revised from previous product and includes a Novice and an Expert Quick Start Guide. Also includes an interactive tutorial on CD-ROM that guides students through an intro to MIDI hardware and software, and a tutorial of ConcertWare titled 'How I Wrote My Fifth Symphony with ConcertWare by Ludwig van Beethoven.' Macintosh requires System 7.0 or higher, 68020 processor or better, and hard drive. Windows requires 386 or faster, sound card or MIDI interface. CD-ROM player required for tutorials."

I deal with ConcertWare next because of its simplicity of use and extremely modest price. This program is not intended for the production of publishable scores, owing to the limited adjustment of such items as slurs and beam angles; still, it is an easy tool for someone who wants a quick playback of a musical idea, and it produces a good-looking and highly readable printed page. Note entry follows the magic piano metaphor—click on an on-screen piano keyboard and the note chosen miraculously appears on the staff. Continuing to click on the appropriate note causes it to be drawn on the staff at the *insertion point,* a winking vertical line that shows you where you are on the apparently endless staff. A chord entry mode can be chosen, but the notes of the chord will all have the same value. Chords with different note lengths have to be entered a different way by identifying different voices. The note duration is chosen either with the mouse or by key equivalent. This type of entry, where notes are entered one at a time, is known as *step entry.* As an alternative to the on-screen piano, a column of whole notes is drawn at the left of the screen with staves and Cs shown as landmarks.

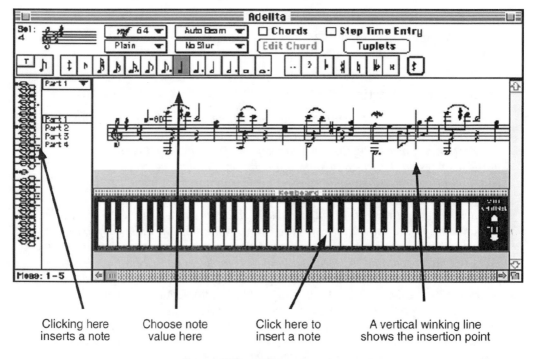

| Clicking here inserts a note | Choose note value here | Click here to insert a note | A vertical winking line shows the insertion point |

ConcertWare: The main screen

As always, the initial setting-up seems the hardest part until it becomes familiar. As I wanted a single staff, I needed to set this up with the ruler as illustrated below.

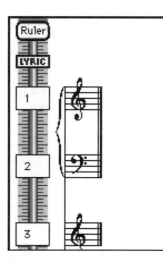

ConcertWare: The ruler used for organizing staves and systems

To obtain my single staff I clicked on the button designated "Ruler," and the following appeared:

Connectors	Parts on Staff				Show	
{ [| 1	Part 1				☒	**Lyric Lines:**
☒☐☒ 2	Part 2				☒	
☐☐☐ 3	Part 3				☒	**1**
☐☐☐ 4	Part 4				☒	
☐☐☐ 5	Part 5				☒	
☐☐☐ 6	Part 6				☒	
☐☐☐ 7	Part 7				☒	
☐☐☐ 8	Part 8				☒	
☐☐☐ 9	Part 9				☐	
☐☐☐ 10	Part 10				☐	
☐☐☐ 11	Part 11				☐	
☐☐☐ 12	Part 12				☐	
☐☐☐ 13	Part 13				☐	Name
☐☐☐ 14	Part 14				☐	Staves
☐☐☐ 15	Part 15				☐	Cancel
☐☐☐ 16	Part 16				☐	OK

Displaying Staves: ◉ 1-16 ○ 17-32

ConcertWare: Adjusting the initial setup

I clicked off the *X*s for "Connectors," since I didn't need these, and on the right-hand side under "Show" I clicked off all but the uppermost box. I decided to make Tarrega's "Adelita" my test piece, to get an idea of how many operations were involved. After first trying to enter chords and single notes, I quickly found out that the bass note could not be made to sustain, since it would have the same time value as the eighth note in the melody. To allow for the different values it was necessary to enter the music in separate parts. Returning to the setup panel, I found that the blank spaces on the first line could be assigned to different parts. Click in the blank area and a drop-down menu appears.

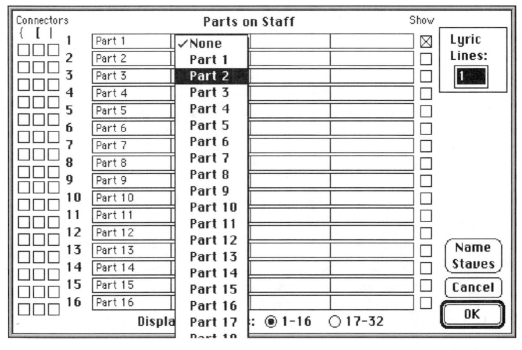

ConcertWare: Assigning voices

I tried to make the Lyric Line box a zero, since there is no lyric, but received a protest when I clicked on OK, so returned and made it a one again. Then I clicked on the top line in the box immediately to the right of "part 1" and the menu appeared, giving me a choice of parts. Having chosen part 2 for this box, I went on to the third space and did the same for part 3. The box now looked like this:

Connectors	Parts on Staff				Show	
{ [| 1	Part 1	Part 2	Part 3		☒	Lyric
□□□ 2					□	Lines:
□□□ 3					□	
□□□ 4					□	

ConcertWare: A single staff with three-voice capability

After clicking OK I was now back to my starting point, almost ready to enter notes. I had forgotten one thing—guitar music should have the clef with an eight underneath so as to tell the computer to play back the music an octave lower than the visible staff. Under the Insert menu I dragged down to the word "clef" and was offered a selection of clefs, including the guitar one.

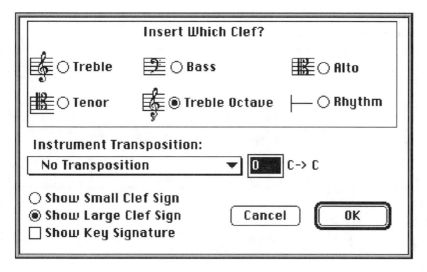

ConcertWare: Selecting a clef

After choosing the clef I was almost ready to start entering notes. Four more choices had to be made: the key signature, the time signature, a choice of how beaming was to be done, and a tempo setting.

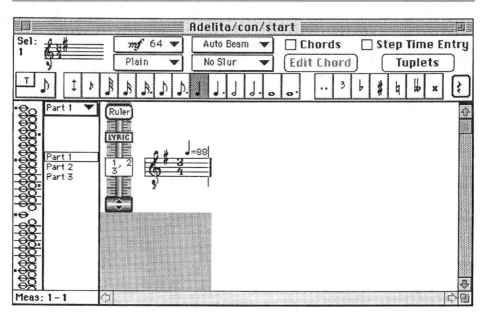

ConcertWare: Ready to start entering guitar score

With the preliminaries out of the way, I began to enter the upper voice, selecting eighth notes and clicking on the piano keyboard. I soon found that I had to click on notes an octave lower, presumably so the computer would later play back the correct pitch. I had a little trouble

ConcertWare: Slurring notes

confining the slur to the correct notes until I found the best way: enter the notes without slurs, then go back and select them by dragging the cursor across them. With the right notes selected, go up to the slur box and click/drag downward until the right slur is found. Let go of the mouse button, and the selected notes are slurred.

After completing the first line, I selected the third part by clicking on its box, then returned to the beginning to enter the bass line. Finally I entered the remaining notes into the second part, and my line looked like this.

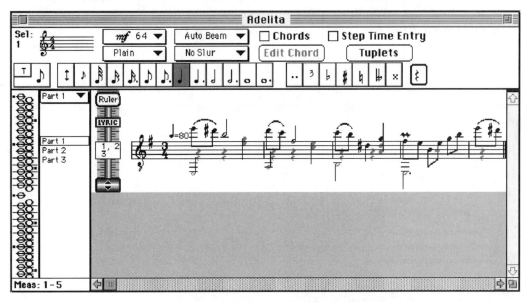

ConcertWare: "Adelita," line 1 complete

The stem directions were not those of the original, but these are easily reversed by selection and key stroke.

Here is a printout of the work so far:

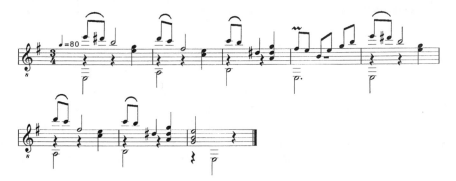

ConcertWare. A printout of work in progress

To hear the playback I chose **Play All** from the Sound menu, and back came audible proof of my entry. With some juggling I was able to hear three sound versions, one from my Macintosh's basic internal sound, a second from the Quicktime player installed in my Mac system, and finally from an external synthesizer.

To get the right sound to come through my synthesizer I used a separate program, InstrumentMaker, supplied with the ConcertWare package. In addition to routing a correct instrument setting to my synthesizer, the program offered some sophisticated sound adjustments. Choosing an individual instrument enabled the sound to be tried out by clicking on the keyboard, and the results of changes made could also be heard.

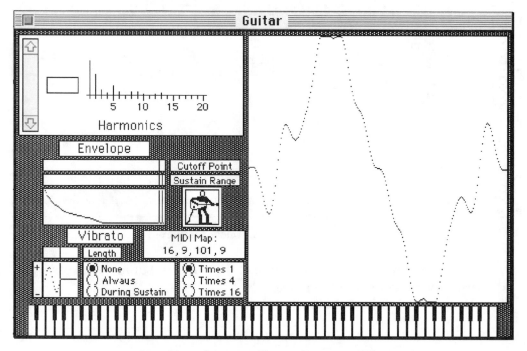

Sound/envelope page from InstrumentMaker

With its extremely moderate price, ConcertWare will be found invaluable for those who want to enter music relatively quickly and hear the playback. This becomes a good practice device when one is learning a piece, since entering the music involves a close study of the score, and the final result may be used as a unison play-along. Alternatively, those working on a song accompaniment or duet can enter the other part and practice with it. There are many opportunities to learn more about MIDI, including real-time recording from a MIDI controller (keyboard or MIDI guitar) if you have one. But if you simply want to hear what some printed notes sound like, ConcertWare's step entry is simple to use. You can print readable score from ConcertWare even though the company makes no claim to engraver or publication status.

ConcertWare is a program packed with features and with a well thought out and clear interface. Although each stage takes some learning and there are moments of frustration, the well-written manual covers most topics well. The CD-ROM tutorial serves as a further guide.

MORE FEATURES, MORE SOPHISTICATION

ENCORE

Passport Designs
100 Stone Pine Road
Half Moon Bay, California 94019
Macintosh or PC

Manufacturer's Description:

"Encore lets you compose, edit, and print music with quick transcription capabilities, powerful tools, and flexible page layout control. Encore transcribes standard notation from your live performance or from standard MIDI files. Step-enter difficult passages with a mouse or MIDI keyboard. Play your score back via MIDI instruments or sound cards. Features include cross-staff beaming, rhythm and percussion staves, automatic transcription of guitar tablature, and playback of dynamic markings, repeats, and multiple endings. Fine-tune your score with symbols, lyrics, text, and guitar chord fret diagrams. Then print your score or individual parts transposed for different instruments. Encore is a professional-level transcription product; it is used as the exclusive choice by MCA/Universal. It is quick, accurate, intuitive, and the most powerful transcription tool on the market. New features include: Customizable Toolbar, Percussion Staff, Zoom, Improved Guessing, OMS Support."

Encore, a popular program from Passport Designs, presents a score page that follows the multiline format rather than the single staff that extends infinitely to the right. The latter is available as an option, however.

After starting the program I was presented with a piano two-staff page, which of course was not what I wanted. Clicking on **New** in the file menu brought up the choices for my initial page.

Setting up for Encore

After the above selections were made, this was the appearance of my page:

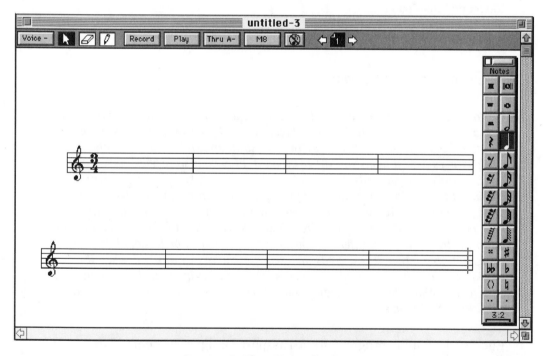

Encore: Setting up a guitar page

The necessary score elements are displayed on a *palette*, which is movable to any part of the screen (here it is on the right). The palette is switched to show more choices by clicking in the area marked "Notes" in this example.

Following the clear manual, I managed to enter the first line of "Adelita," though not without some false starts. I found the slurs hard to handle until I discovered the convenient zoom feature, which enlarges a section of the screen. In the enlarged area I was able to adjust the beginning, middle, and end points of the slurs for optimum appearance.

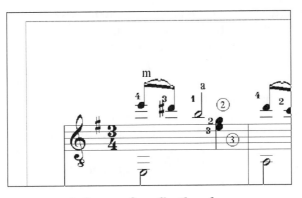

A close-up for adjusting slurs

The Guitar palette offered handy fingering symbols and a quick way to draw bar indications. *P, i, m,* and *a* were available for right-hand fingering, and left-hand fingers were available through the Symbols palette. The eventual result looked like this:

"Adelita," in Encore

Tablature with Encore

One part of Encore that I found intriguing was its ability to make tablature. Again some false starts and adjustments had to be made, but eventually all was well and the result was as shown above. You may select part or all of the page, then click on the menu item **Make Tab.** Encore will attempt to intabulate what you have selected. Obviously, there are many possible renderings, and the first attempt is unlikely to be entirely correct. However, there is an easy system whereby a tab number may be *nudged* from one string to another, with the corresponding change of fret being made automatically. For instance, a zero on the first string may be pulled down to the second string, at which point it changes into a five. In addition, you may specify the lowest fret to be used in a selected passage, which forces intabulation to a certain area of the guitar fingerboard.

In the example above, the B in the third measure was interpreted by **Make Tab** as being on the fifth string, whereas it needs to be on the sixth. The first step was to drag over the number to select it.

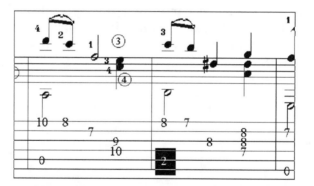

Encore: "Adelita" with tablature before editing

Now it was possible to choose the command **Nudge Down** from the edit menu. This moved the number to the sixth string and changed it automatically from two to seven.

Encore includes the usual MIDI facilities and will make notation from some types of imported MIDI file. A sample MIDI file comes with the program, the familiar Bach Two-Part Invention in A Minor, and Encore converts this from MIDI to notation as a demonstration. The results in this case are (predictably) excellent. Some other conversions are less faithful to sustained notes and have spelling problems (E flat instead of D sharp, for instance), but in general this is an acceptable starting point, and the many available editing features make it eventually possible to finish a score in the preferred form.

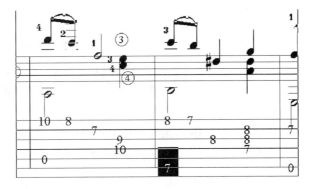

"Adelita" in tab, after editing

Scores can also be created by playing the piece in from a keyboard or guitar controller, and the usual quantizing (setting the minimum note value) and some other note-guessing abilities help to avoid the unreadable mess that usually comes from unvarnished performances.

Here is the printed version:

Adelita

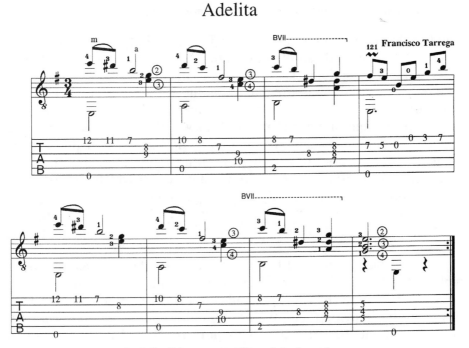

"Adelita" in Encore: The printed version

NIGHTINGALE

Musicware
Temporal Acuity Products
300 120th Ave. NE, Bldg. 1
Bellevue, Washington 98005

This full-featured program is the creation of Don Byrd, an acknowledged notation expert, and has been refined over many years. Here is how the manual describes it:

"Nightingale is a powerful, MIDI-compatible desktop publishing program used to create, edit, and print publication-quality musical scores. It is designed with four basic goals in mind:

1. *To provide 'one-stop' desktop music publishing—a single user at a single computer can create, finish, and publish his/her scores to a worldwide audience, either on paper or electronically over the Internet.*

2. *To provide extreme flexibility—you, as the composer/arranger, are allowed to create anything you want.*

3. *To be a fast and intuitive tool for quickly notating music, while staying out of the way of your creative instincts.*

4. *To create the highest quality of PostScript output available."*

Nightingale presents a considerable challenge at first, partly owing to the amount and level of detail of the documentation, and partly owing to the sheer number of options. There are some unusual shortcuts to speed up note entry, including a *Mouse Shake* routine where a sideways back and forth shake at a user-adjustable rate will return you to a commonly used editing arrow, and another shake back to whatever tool you were using before. This kind of imaginative programming helps negotiation through what might at first seem a rather daunting range of capabilities. The user's manual has more than six hundred pages, of which approximately the last third is an alphabetically arranged reference section.

The basic working area is conveniently laid out, with a large and comprehensive palette that can be further increased by clicking in the top right corner.

The "Adelita" entry went fairly smoothly after the discovery of how to replace the piano staff with a single guitar line. The slurs are quite easy to draw—you click on the first note and the slur draws automatically to the next one—but moving them to a position above the beam took considerable adjustment. Unfortunately, this adjustment did not hold through another operation, and the first line had to be done again. However, I imagine this to be an unusual situation.

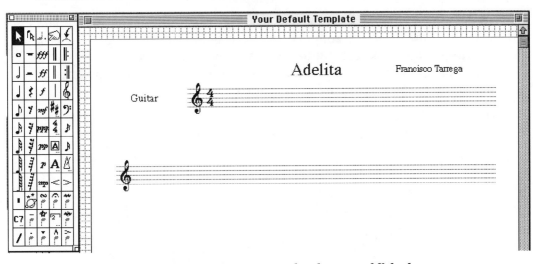

Nightingale: My startup page has been established

Nightingale is not especially friendly to the guitar, having for instance no palette-entered *p, i, m, a* fingering or barré signs. Nor does it attempt to deal with tablature. Entry of guitar music involves the identification and separate entry of different voices, and the instruction for fingerboard diagrams reads "Create these using the Text Tool, and select Text Style 3 (which is Sonata) and then use Sonata Font and build the guitar diagrams

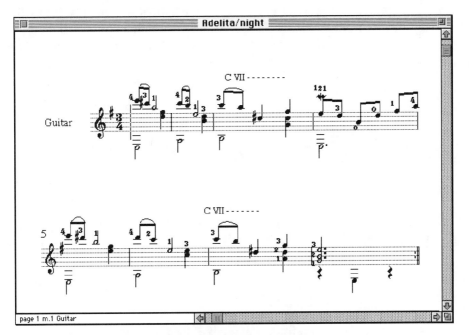

Nightingale: Setting "Adelita"

one step at a time." Hardly spoon-feeding, especially since the Sonata PostScript font was not supplied in the original package. Nonetheless, Nightingale has good capabilities for full score, playback, part extraction from scores, and sophisticated transposition avoiding the misspellings of sharps and flats so common in other programs.

Adelita

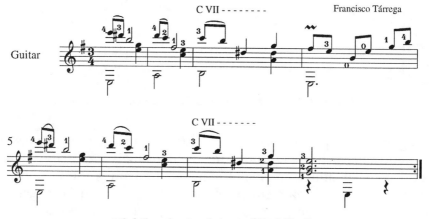

Nightingale: A printout of "Adelita"

Nightingale will make as good a guess as most at an imported MIDI file. Here is a sample piece by S. L. Weiss, published as a MIDI file by MIDI Classics of Simsbury, Connecticut, from *The Baroque Guitar* (Ariel Music Publications). First, the original publication:

An extract from "Passacaille" by S. L. Weiss

Here is how the MIDI file was interpreted by Nightingale after transposition up an octave.

Nightingale: Interpretation of a MIDI file

Further information about Nightingale can be found in connection with the NoteScan Optical Character Recognition feature, discussed in chapter 5.

OVERTURE

Opcode Systems, Inc.
3950 Fabian Way, Suite 100
Palo Alto, California 94303

Opcode's Overture is easier to use than some of the other high-end programs. Here is an extract from what the manufacturer claims for it:

"Overture's publishing features are on a par with those found in the best professional page layout programs. All objects can be scaled, zoomed in and out on, and nudged one pixel at a time with arrow keys. Overture has extensive text-handling capabilities for lyrics, text boxes, rehearsal marks, and footers and headers. For even more publishing ease, EPS files can be created from any area of the score.

Some of Overture's outstanding features include:

- *Faster and easier to use than any other notation package.*
- *Page Layout Mode for precision editing of all elements.*
- *MIDI Editing including Opcode's famous graphic window with Strip Chart.*
- *Instant access to all tools, without changing modes.*
- *Drag over any section of a score to create a PICT or EPS file."*

Naturally, I was interested in the "faster and easier notation" claim, so I set about entering my test lines as before.

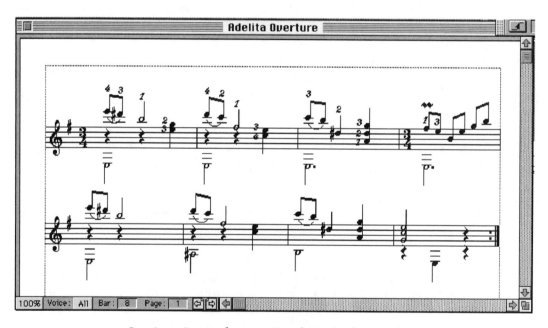

Overture: As usual, separate voice entry is necessary

As it turned out, note entry was quite convenient except for the inevitable necessity of entering notes by separate voice. A switch at the bottom of the screen toggled between the various voices. Stem directions were usually wrong for contrapuntal setting until corrected with a menu choice, and sometimes seemed to revert to their original appearance following other editing operations. Slurs went in easily—the notes to be slurred were selected by dragging with the mouse after the type of slur was chosen from a palette. Fingerings were also chosen from a palette, but unfortunately there was no 0 for the open string, nor could I find indications for the barré, such as Roman numerals, or numbers in circles to indicate strings. This lack more or less rules out Overture as a publishing vehicle for the classical guitarist.

Tablature in Overture

Tablature is possible in Overture. The first step in a multistage process is to enter notes on the appropriate strings to indicate time values on the tablature staff.

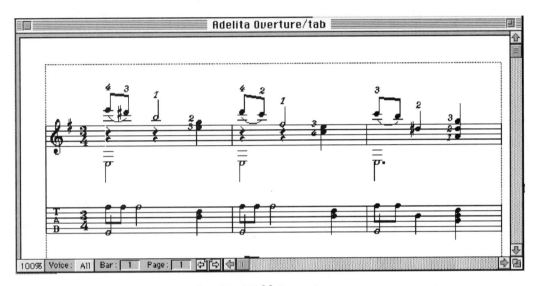

Overture: Tablature, stage one

The next step is to choose numbers from a palette. You have to decide which numbers, since there is no element of translation. The numbers are then clicked onto the noteheads. Finally, the stems are removed with a menu command, leaving the plain tablature. On the whole, this was a cumbersome process compared to the automatic features of Encore.

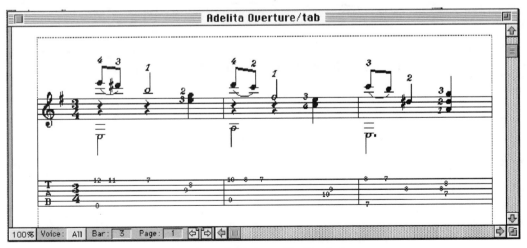

Overture: Tablature, the final stage

Overture made a reasonably good guess at our sample MIDI file. A dialog box offered the choice of single- or two-staff transcription and single or multiple voices. However, when multiple voices were transcribed to a single staff, the erratic stem directions made the score highly confusing. Transcription to a single voice (illustrated) was easier to read though less informative. When two-staff transcription was chosen, the multiple voices were well handled.

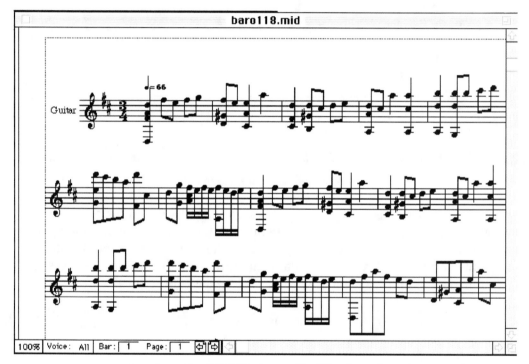

Overture: The MIDI file transcribed for the guitar

Overture: The MIDI file on two staves

Adelita

Francisco Tárrega

Overture: A printout of "Adelita" in progress

Overture: A printout of the tablature version

FINALE

Coda Music Technology
6210 Bury Dr.
Eden Prairie, Minnesota 55346–1718

Finale is an impressive program that claims to be the last one that you will need, be you composer, arranger, or performer. It comes with three mighty volumes of manual, more than 850 pages in all; considerable study is clearly needed to master all that can be done. Early versions were much criticized for an overcomplex approach, with dialog boxes that led to more and more dialog boxes. just to perform a simple operation. Fortunately, this criticism resulted in a radical redesign of the interface, with much more on the visible surface, and a major rewrite of the manuals, so today's Finale and its younger sibling, Finale Allegro, are definitely more approachable than the original publication.

The page can be viewed as an endless staff or in page format, which I normally prefer. Initial layout is perhaps more time-consuming than with some other programs. I wanted a broadly spaced single-staff page, about six lines to a page, with plenty of space at top and bottom. Much of this layout seemed to be the province of the Staff Tool, which unfortunately was not accessible in the format that I was using. I decided to open a *template*—one of the predesigned pages supplied with the program—and found that the only option was one called Lead Sheet. This was really too closely spaced for "Adelita," but I used it anyway. At least it only had one staff, and I was not stuck impotently trying to erase other lines.

A particularly important and useful feature of the workscreen is the brief explanation at the top of the screen of the tool that you have chosen—in this case, the zoom tool for enlarging the work area.

Note entry from the palette was simple. Note values were chosen from the palette and plopped into place on the staff with a crossed-hairs type of cursor that made aiming easy. Slurring was accomplished without too much difficulty. When it came to entering fingering, however, a long and tedious process of defining numbers from a selected font and installing them in a dialog box intervened before the simplest entry was possible. When that was done, placing the finger number correctly involved a series of selections, clicks, and drags. Entering a rest also seemed over-complicated, although, as with many of these processes, one realized that familiarity would make a difference.

Finale: Setting "Adelita"

To enter the guitar bar indication (CVII—in this case) involved making a text box and then attaching it to an individual measure or to the page. It certainly can be done, and no doubt with familiarity the process becomes easier. But at first the whole fingering process was tedious and time-consuming.

Tablature with Finale

Tablature can be set up in Finale for virtually any instrument by making a single-line ministaff for each string. The instructions are somewhat daunting: "Repeat the last eight steps (beginning with the instruction marked by the ⅝) for this second (one-line) staff. Repeat the entire process for the remaining 'staff lines' of the tablature staff, remembering to enter an appropriate Base Key (open string) for each." Of course, this sounds worse out of context, and fortunately for the guitarist Finale comes with a ready-made template for standard guitar tablature, but the tablature conversion in no way compares to the elegant and rapid process offered by Encore.

For the "Adelita" example I decided to use the template. I had to widen the space between the tab and regular staff, but this was easily achieved by dragging, using the staff tool. Next I copied and pasted the music from my completed "Adelita" sample.

My first attempt was not very successful. The paste into my tablature setup of the first measure was transposed by a third, so I had to start by repositioning it. Then, when I dragged the notes down to the tab staff, which is the way they are converted to numbers, the fingerings came down as well, being attached to the notes. The result was chaotic, so the next step was to remove the fingerings. I couldn't seem to do this on the tab staff, so I went back to square one and cleaned the fingerings off the original music.

Now I was ready to start. Three measures of "Adelita" had been copied over, and the music staff now had a correct (guitar) clef corresponding to the original music. The time signature had also been adjusted. I first dragged the bass note down to the bottom string. Nothing happened. Then I dragged the highest note to the first string, and a zero appeared, denoting an open string. Since the note was at the twelfth fret, something was obviously wrong. Because the guitar clef transposes an octave, the tablature was doing the same. The bottom note had not transcribed because it was out of range. Now what? Presumably change the clef to a standard one. This I did, and found my music transposed down an octave. Becoming now quite good at transposition, I put it back to the correct octave and tried again.

This time I was more successful. The notes in the first two measures transcribed correctly, and all seemed fine. Then in the third measure trouble arose, since the computer insisted that the D sharp, which I wanted on the third string, was an open string instead of at the eighth fret. At this point I gave up and printed out what had already been entered. To my surprise the erroneous open string printed as an eight, that is, correctly. Encouraged by this, I continued the process. After copying in the remaining score measures and accomplishing the transposition (becoming faster with practice), I was able to make tablature for the remainder of the extract. So—writing tab in Finale is anything but fast, but it can be done. Although on the screen it is hard to distinguish the 8 from the 0 when on the line, the printout is clear.

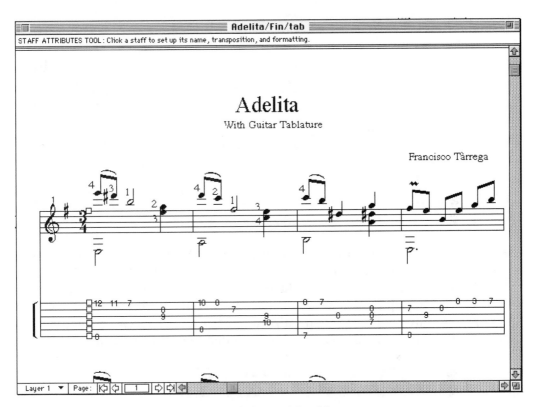

Finale: "Adelita" with tablature

Finale's MIDI entry

As well as a full range of standard sequencing features, Finale has a most useful and simple way to enter notes from a MIDI keyboard or controller. You beat time using an assigned key or control on your keyboard, and this becomes the control beat for the computer. This allows for slowing down and speeding up at will and avoids the pressure associated with playing to a metronome. This can be considered as a halfway house between entering the notes one by one and real-time performance.

Finale does a good job of importing MIDI files from other programs, although the setup instructions could be clearer.

Finale: Transcription from the MIDI file.

Here the same MIDI test file is transcribed by Finale. For some reason, at the first attempt the first measure was spread over the whole line, but using the menu command **Update Layout** reformatted the page as shown. The interpretation on two staves was better in terms of the sustaining of individual parts. Requesting a guitar staff produced an interpretation of the file with considerable loss of individual voice information.

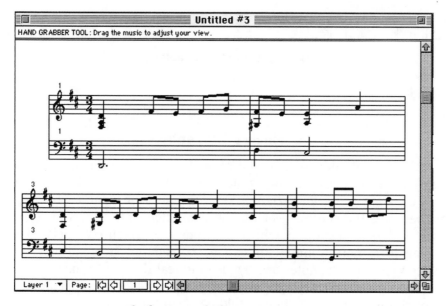

Finale: Transcription on two staves

Perhaps the best thing about Finale for the guitarist with limited MIDI experience or interest is the quality of the final printed music. The quality is up to publication standard; in fact, Finale's output is quite widely used commercially. Using it is like having a huge bag of tools, where inevitably the one you want is at the bottom of the bag. But all those tools give you much capability, and if you have the time and the patience, the final result can be excellent.

Adelita
With Guitar Tablature

Francisco Tàrrega

Finale: A printed page

MOSAIC

Mark of the Unicorn
1280 Massachusetts Ave.
Cambridge, Massachusetts 02138

Manufacturer's description:

"State-of-the-art music desktop publishing software for the Macintosh. Provides a WYSIWYG environment in which you can produce publication-quality music notation, from lead sheets to full orchestra scores. Includes real-time MIDI recording and playback, as well as convenient step-record and mouse and keyboard note entry.

Supports standard MIDI file format. Unlimited voices, staves, and voices per staff. Unlimited Undo/Redo. Unique multiple views feature—see the same music formatted differently in separate windows, such as a transposed staff in an instrument part and the same staff at a smaller point size in concert pitch in the conductor score—all in the same file and linked dynamically. (Drag a note in one window, for example, and it changes in the others.) Completely flexible page formatting directly on the page. Precise, flexible, 'click-and-drag' placement of over 160 musical symbols. Reshape slurs, ties, dynamics, and more. Word-processing-style lyric entry with automatic text flow through music. Advanced features include engraver spacing, cross-staff beaming, all forms of musical transposition, check rhythm and range commands, and complex meters."

WYSIWYG, incidentally, stands for "what you see is what you get," meaning that when you print your page it will resemble closely what you are looking at on the screen. One tends to take that for granted nowadays.

I found Mosaic to have many good features, reflecting the experience gained by Mark of the Unicorn after many years in the field. Their Profes-

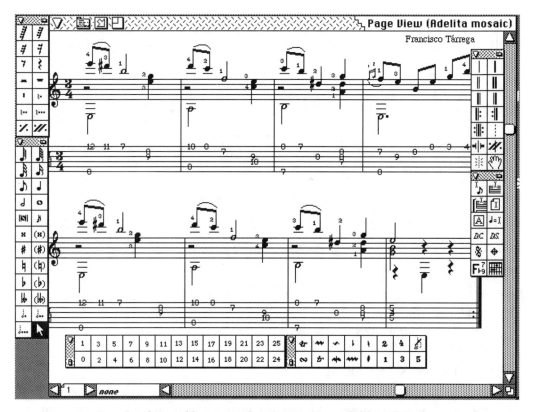

Mosaic: The working area, showing some available palettes

Adelita

for Guitar

Francisco Tárrega

Mosaic: A printed page

sional Composer was one of the first composition/scoring/MIDI programs on the market, and Mosaic reflects many improvements suggested by users of that program. Among features I particularly liked was the sophisticated Undo mechanism—the ability to step backward, undoing the previous steps. I also liked the easy cut-and-paste features natural to Macintosh graphic programs and the easy placing and erasing of symbols including fingering. The arrow cursor showing at the bottom of the Notes palette was an invaluable tool for most graphic editing functions, including the fine-tuning of note and fingering symbols by a simple select-and-drag process.

Interpretation of the sample MIDI file was not a strong feature, owing to the misspelling of accidentals (A flat for G sharp, etc.) and the setting of long notes as many short notes tied together. This was rather a surprise in a program with so many good features.

The tablature construction was virtually the same as the procedure described above for Overture—usable but a bit cumbersome. A nice feature was the ability to adjust the size of the final tablature numbers for printing, necessary because the on-screen numbers are too small for practical use. This same feature would have been nice if applied to the conventional fingering numbers. I was disappointed to find that the readily available palettes did not contain the string or barré indications for the guitar, nor was a zero provided for open strings. Presumably something could be done with text boxes and other fonts, but this would be far less convenient than just including the items in one of the palettes. Perhaps a future version of this otherwise excellent program will address this problem, and thus make it more guitar friendly.

MUSICATOR

P.O. Box 73793
Davis, California 95617

Musicator, for the PC, is an extremely comprehensive program by Jo Brodtkorb of Norway, which includes multitrack MIDI recording with very extensive facilities, audio direct-to-disk recording, mixing of audio and MIDI tracks, and so on, at a very competitive price. It also handles notation well, though not pretending to be an engraver's program. For instance, of all the programs in which I tested an imported standard MIDI file, Musicator produced the best initial version on a single staff—in fact, the only one that came close to the original score.

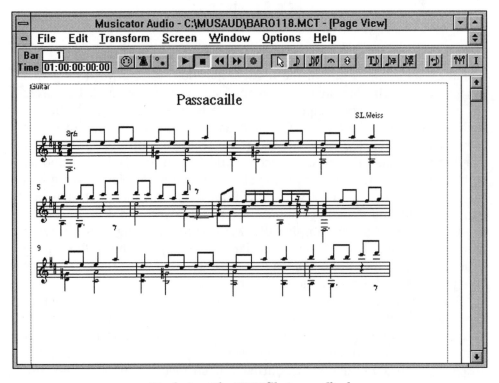

Musicator: The MIDI file transcribed

It was necessary to convert the initial reading from piano to single staff, since this choice was not available prior to transcription. It was a simple menu choice after the event, however, and as stated, the result was among the best.

The "Adelita" example was not entered, since the program's strength lies more in its handling of MIDI and audio recordings, the notation facilities being more focused on editing scores produced by MIDI entry. Most necessary features, such as slurs, dynamics, and so forth, were available, but not the guitar-specific indications for strings or barré.

CONCLUSIONS

For me, a notation program is interesting only if it will save me time and do exactly what I want. While enjoying the proofreading assistance of audible MIDI playback, I hate having to enter guitar music as separate voices, since most classical guitar music has contrapuntal voices that appear and disappear. As one tries to separate the lines, the score becomes cluttered with additional rests. In general, the voice-by-voice approach is not what I want. Similarly, I am not particularly interested in entering notes via a MIDI controller. The reason is that in any kind of finished work the notes are really only a small part of the necessary entries for guitar music; there are fingerings, bar signs, string indications, harmonics, slides, and so on, and I may want tablature as well. As a result, I find it faster to work directly with the score, and for me the simplicity of the entry features is the most important element. It was for this reason that SpeedScore was designed, and it remains, for me at least, by far the fastest and easiest way to create a publishable classical guitar score.

Nevertheless the high-end programs have fine features, and sometimes it is worth the annoyance of voice entry to access those features. For composers there is obviously a tremendous advantage to having the MIDI facility, particularly when the composition includes other instruments. Another convenience is the use of MIDI playback for play-along practice. It is useful to be able to hear your partner's duet part or a vocal part that you plan to accompany. MIDI also has an advantage over live recording in that you can slow down or speed up the tempo without altering the pitch.

Another worthwhile feature for many will be Encore's tablature-making capability. A student who is a poor reader may enter the piece he is studying and convert it to tablature. As a teacher I would tend to regard this use of tablature as a crutch that would slow down the learning of standard notation. However, the act of entering the score, with the need to identify the voices, is itself a lesson in notation, and the inevitable corrections to automatically generated tablature constitute another lesson in looking closely at the score. After a few conversions of this type many students would no doubt tire of the work and decide that it is really easier just to study the conventional notation. But there is always some beginner who is determined to learn a piece like Albeniz's "Leyenda" by sheer drive and determination, and while he or she probably won't play the piece any sooner, the exercise may well be worthwhile.

Part extraction is a handy feature for those who need it. In fact for the professional copyist or composer of orchestral scores the ability to print out separate parts is of major importance. For the guitarist it is less so, usually involving no more than a duet or vocal part. This can be accomplished in SpeedScore by simple cutting and pasting, but other programs give the opportunity for layout adjustment and easy automated processes. How important this is to you will depend on your primary use for a scoring program.

Finale and Nightingale both offer a wide range of features, and Nightingale is currently the only Mac program to offer the scanning in and recognition of printed music, a subject dealt with in detail in chapter 5. But both suffer from the inevitable complexity that arises from programs with large numbers of dialog boxes to access the myriad features. They are not for the neophyte, and both involve a considerable learning period.

For the PC platform, Leland Smith's Score has fine professional capabilities, but is undoubtedly the hardest to master, owing to the command-driven (as opposed to mouse-driven) entry system. It has an excellent reputation, but is not recommended to the amateur.

Encore, from Passport Designs, and Overture, from Opcode, are easier to approach, with good documentation and not as Byzantine an approach to the user interface. Of the two, I preferred Encore for the guitarist, since the special symbols and tablature creation were better. Basic entry was of comparable difficulty between the two.

Cakewalk Professional, which appears in chapter 4 in connection with audio recording, is an excellent MIDI sequencing program with some scoring facilities but with no real pretensions to engraving and publication. The note entry process is not well suited to solo guitar music, and the strengths of this popular program lie in other areas, such as the easy creation and playback of complex MIDI sequences and the editing of audio material. In this regard it comes into the same category as Musicator.

With so much careful programming and so many features available, it becomes of paramount importance to define your specific need and to understand how much of that need can be met by using a given program. Then it is necessary to compare the actual handling of the various programs to see which seems practical to use in the chosen areas. Fortunately, the availability of free demonstration programs helps the evaluation process greatly, and in spite of the tedium of installation and initial learning, this is the best possible way to find the right program for your particular needs.

FOUR
DIRECT-TO-DISK RECORDING

I should begin by saying that direct-to-disk recording is not as simple as plugging a microphone into a tape recorder. Some of the easier approaches are described below, and those with a strong technical bent will probably enjoy experimenting in this area, but professional recording is quite demanding and the reader with this in mind may want to look ahead to the conclusions at the end of this chapter.

THE BASICS OF DIGITAL RECORDING

When audio is recorded on a tape deck, the impulses from the microphone magnetize the tape in a linear way; that is, the audio signal is recorded on the tape in a straight line from beginning to end. Playback consists of passing the tape over the playback head, again in a linear fashion. When the playback is completed, the tape must be rewound before it can be played again. Similarly, to move to any particular segment of the recording the tape must be wound forward or back—a time-consuming process.

In recording to a hard disk, data that has been converted to a stream of ones and zeroes are "written" by the record/playback head to tracks on a fast-spinning disk. The whole process is so fast that the head can jump almost instantaneously to any part of the disk, virtually eliminating the waiting time for rewinding or fast-forwarding.

In addition to this time-saving process, often referred to as *random access*, the hard disk offers the tremendous advantage of nondestructive editing. To take a practical example, if you have made a splendid take of a piece of music but the sound is spoiled at one point by the ugly sound of a fingernail contacting the string, normally you would prefer to keep the good take but somehow eliminate the bad sound. With a conventional tape recording the traditional method would be to cut the piece out by skillful physical editing, which involves manually rocking the tape back and forth over the playback head to find the exact in and out spots. In making the cut you might miss the ideal place, and the whole take could end up on the cutting room floor. The process has now involved both time and aggravation.

In contrast, the hard disk, with its random access, enables you to simulate the cut and hear the result in advance of saving the final version. Great accuracy can be assured, since the cut place can be selected down to the millisecond, and if it isn't right you simply do it again without any danger to the original recording. When you play back your cut version the computer is able to arrive at the cut point, skip to the "out" point, and continue playing. When you eventually are happy with the finished version, it can be copied to a new file that has exactly the same fidelity as the original. On a tape recorder you would be worried that the copy had "lost a generation," that is, deteriorated slightly in the copying process. But here lies one of the tremendous advantages of digital recording—copying should make no alteration at all, since all that is copied is a series of numbers, and the absolute correctness of the copy can be verified by the computer. As a result, the many parts of a multi-instrument recording can be built into a final mix with no difference in any instrument from the original, first-generation recording. In addition, sections may be repeated, or the order of sections rearranged, by a simple cutting-and-pasting process. In every case the result can be approved before the final finished product is saved.

There are some interesting possibilities for the experimenter. For instance, you can create a chorus effect with a vocal passage by placing it in four separate tracks and slightly offsetting the audio in each track.

Unfortunately, as has been mentioned, there is a price to be paid for direct-to-disk recording in the cost of the recording medium. One minute of monaural audio takes up approximately 5 megabytes (Mb) of space on your hard disk. Double that for stereo and a minute uses up 10 Mb. Fortunately the cost of large (1,000 Mb and more) drives has come down dramatically, so for the hobbyist the cost will probably be an acceptable one-time investment. Those who wish to record large groups with multiple takes, however, can fill up a gigabyte (1,000 megabyte) drive very quickly. For more professional use the compromise of a digital tape recorder (usually called a DAT recorder) for the original recordings prior to editing will usually be preferable. DAT recorders can be used in conjunction with computers so that the operations are integrated by the software.

SIMPLE RECORDING ON THE MAC

On both Macintosh and PC computers it is fairly simple to make a voice or guitar recording without extra equipment beyond the basic sound card. As mentioned, the PC has no innate musical capability, but almost all PCs are now sold with a sound add-on good enough to play music from the built-in CD-ROM drives that are now almost standard. Modern Macs come with an audio system sophisticated enough to record digital sound onto the hard disk at sample rates of CD quality. The sample rate is the amount of times per second that the audio input is measured and converted into a numeric value (i.e., digitized), a higher rate producing better quality. On the computer that I am using, a 7600/120 Power Macintosh, two sample rates are offered for music, 44.1 and 22.05 kiloherz. The lower figure uses less disk space. The computer came with an Apple PlainTalk microphone, which may be directly plugged into the back of the computer for simple recording. In addition, Apple's Quicktime and Quicktime Musical Instruments system extensions provide for playback of MIDI tracks.

A menu choice called SimpleSound starts a simple program for recording. I tried this out after plugging in the Apple microphone. Selecting **New** from SimpleSound's File menu brought up a picture of a standard control device.

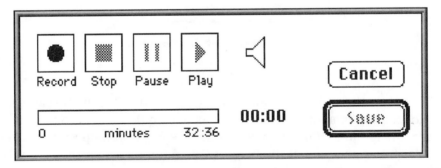

The Macintosh SimpleSound control panel

I positioned the microphone on top of the monitor, as recommended by the manual, and started the recording by clicking on **Record**. The number at the bottom showed me, in minutes and seconds of playback time, how much space was available for the recording on my hard drive. I cautiously played in about thirty seconds of guitar music.

Next I clicked on **Play** and waited for the playback. There wasn't any, but with the help of the manual I found that I had failed to open the Monitors and Sound Control panel and to select the microphone as the audio input device. After making the correct choice I tried again.

I played back the first attempt through the internal system and found the output somewhat anemic in volume and with a noticeably scratchy background. The background disappeared on silent segments, producing a rather disturbing coming and going. Clearly this was not going to work for quality recording. Returning to SimpleSound, I looked, as I should have before, for further options and found that the default setting was on Music Quality. There was another selection, CD quality, so this time I chose this and repeated the recording.

Choices in Macintosh SimpleSound

This time the difference was dramatic. The unpleasant background was gone, and the sound was as good as one could expect from an inexpensive microphone. Encouraged by this, I plugged in amplified speakers to the appropriate outlet at the back of the computer and played the piece back at normal volume with good results.

Allowing for the delays caused by first-time use, the process was not significantly more difficult than plugging a microphone into a tape recorder. The noise of the computer is more than that of a good tape transport, so arrangements have to be made to increase the distance from it; also, the use of a directional microphone becomes important. The quality of both input and output can be raised to a more professional level, but there are no level controls or editing facilities with Simple-Sound. For these features it becomes necessary to seek out more sophisticated software.

SIMPLE RECORDING ON THE PC

SOUNDBLASTER

Because IBM-compatible PCs do not include sound systems in their basic configuration, it becomes necessary to incorporate a sound card. The expression "card" is used for many of the add-on pieces of equipment that can be plugged into slots inside the case of the computer. The miniature components are usually grouped tightly on a rectangular board at one end of which are the necessary plug connections to fit into the standard slots provided on all PCs. The slot provides the power and access to the main parts of the computer. One of the most popular sound cards, the SoundBlaster from Creative Labs, contains a recording option similar to SimpleSound on the Mac. The installed card provides miniplug sockets for microphone, line in, line out, speakers out, and a game port also used for MIDI in and out.

SoundBlaster's Creative Mixer

Creative Labs
1901 McCarthy Blvd.
Milpitas, California 95035

After a microphone is plugged in, it is necessary to open the Creative Mixer to establish in and out levels. In my setup, the default for the microphone level was "off," so my first attempt to record was again a blank. Then I discovered the mixer and was able to establish the various levels without difficulty. The next step was to double-click on the Soundo'LE icon, which brought up a control panel with a format similar to those on a cassette recorder.

SoundBlaster: Creative Soundo'LE control window

OLE, by the way, has nothing to do with cries of encouragement. It stands for Object Linking and Embedding. This means that sound files made this way can be inserted into and played from other programs. Information on this more advanced topic can be found in the manual for Microsoft Windows.

Operating Soundo'LE is simple. The central part of the display shows the sound levels for each channel. Below it is a slider that shows progress through the sound file. The arrows are, from the left, the conventional ones for play, pause, rewind, fast forward, stop, and record.

Because the input in this case is a single microphone, the result will be a monaural recording, which has the advantage of using half the space of an equivalent stereo track. A guitarist recording practice sessions will find the quality to be better than that of a simple cassette recorder. Stereo recording is still possible, since the *line input* has left and right channels. Line input is for high-impedence, high-level inputs, however, whereas most microphones output low level at low impedence. Apple gets around this problem by making available a *line level* microphone. You don't have to know what impedence is, but you do have to match like to like. For instance, a microphone preamplifier, which takes input from one or more microphones and outputs high-impedence line output, would enable stereo recording on this system. Of course, before you go out to buy a mike preamplifier you need to assess how far you are going to go with this system.

Because the internal speaker in most PCs is totally inadequate for music playback, outboard speakers are recommended. These are now readily available with built-in amplification. A further advantage of this add-on is that music CDs can be played from your computer's CD-ROM drive while other work is being done.

GOING TO THE NEXT LEVEL

While straightforward digital recordings can be made quite simply on both PC and Mac, there is little control of either input or output. What you record is what you get, and if you don't like it there is not much that you can do beyond using a better microphone. To record with optimum level control, and subsequently to manipulate the quality of the track and edit it, requires more complex and more expensive software. More sophisticated programs allow you to optimize the recording level after the event so the volume peaks are exactly the maximum possible before distortion appears—an extremely useful feature known as *normalizing*. A degree of tone manipulation, known generally as *equalization* or EQ, can be applied to the recorded track, but do not expect all programs to have a sophisticated range of sliders throughout the sound spectrum as with analog equalizers. Some offer high pass, low pass, and band pass filters, which attenuate highs, lows, or both, but that's about as elaborate as it gets. Cutting and pasting, however, even down to rearranging the words in a sentence, can be achieved easily and nondestructively, since no tape is actually cut and no material erased until trial edits have been approved. A final take can easily be assembled from multiple takes, and in this regard computer editing is much to be preferred over physical tape cutting.

MORE ADVANCED PC

Actually, a surprising amount of extra sophistication is available from SoundBlaster's included program called Creative WaveStudio. For instance, it is possible to add echo, not available with Studio Vision (see below), and also to do a wide variety of cutting and pasting, volume adjustment, fading in and out, inserting silence, and so on.

As with all such programs, the main interface for these actions is a visual representation of the sound. The chunks of sound produced by notes or chords are conventionally known as *sound events*.

The illustration shows editing views from Creative WaveStudio. I first recorded the first section of the Gaspar Sanz Pavane, and in the lower panel, called the Preview, the complete recording can be seen in a wave

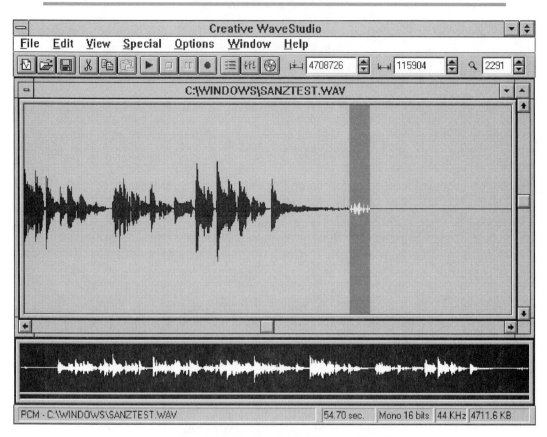

Creative WaveStudio: A visible sound track

representation from left to right, the taller peaks representing louder sounds. From these it is fairly easy to identify the beginning of a new note, because the attack causes a large volume. As the note dies off, the peaks gradually become lower, dwindling down to silence when only the center line shows.

The upper window shows an enlarged section of the piece. The larger size is necessary for accuracy in editing. The places to be altered are selected by dragging the cursor over them. To give a simple example, I selected a cluster of sounds at the very end of the recording, which were actually made by my putting down the guitar and reaching over to stop the recording. Having selected the section, I simply choose **Delete** from the Edit menu, and at this point the corrected file is redrawn. I can then play it to see if it sounds right. If it does, I save the file. If not, I can choose **Undo** from the Edit menu, which in effect restores to the screen the previously saved version. It is important to save frequently as successful edits are made, so the undo does not revert too far.

Looking at the file again, which has now lost the cluster of random sound at the end, I may decide to fade the last note out a little sooner. Again all I have to do is select the area, listen to it a few times (a playback option is conveniently available by pressing the right-hand mouse button), and zero in on the place to fade out. Some simple menu choices, and I have a tidy fade-out where I want it.

In addition, I could select the whole file to add an echo effect. Doing this several times apparently causes a metallic effect, which the documentation promotes as an option. I can't imagine wanting this, so I pass on to *inserting silence*. This quite popular feature involves taking areas of very low level that are intended to be silences, as for instance during a rest, and removing any background noise so as to produce the closest thing possible to actual silence. This has to be done with caution, however, since with a solo instrument the in-and-out effect of the background is noticeable.

MORE ADVANCED MACINTOSH

STUDIO VISION PRO

Opcode Systems Inc.
3950 Fabian Way
Palo Alto, California 94303

I next tried out Studio Vision Pro, a popular program from Opcode Systems that allows direct recording without extra hardware. After following the instructions for enabling the microphone under an audio menu item called Hardware Setup, which brought up the Apple SimpleSound choices, I then chose from the Windows menu one called Record Monitor.

Here the familiar level indicator showed the volume level. If I had checked the Stereo box below the indicators, there would be a white circle beside the Right recording indicators as well as the Left one. In this case, enabling one channel not only saved disk space but also allowed me to try out some editing options not available in stereo. Clicking in the cir-

Record Monitor							
Rec	-45 -26 -10 -2	Clip	Record File		Available	Instrument	
○ Left			▯ (none)			Audio-1	
Right							
Thru: Off		☐ Stereo		☐ Auto Compact	Sample Size: 16 bits		

Studio Vision's Record Monitor

cle next to the Left indicator turned it red, indicating that it was ready to record, and caused a box to appear, requesting a file name for the recording. The next control had the usual start/stop/pause buttons familiar to users of cassette decks.

☐	Overdub ⟷		●	▷	■	▶	❚❚		1 · 1 · 0			↘	1 · 1 · 0
Seq	Sequence A											◢	∞ · ·
Trk	(new track)		◀◀	◀▮▶	▶▶			† 00:00:00:00				↘◢	↩
▦	MT-32-10		1 2 3 4 5 6 7 8					♩ = 120.00 ▭▬					
▦◁	Program ???		⊘ Internal	Countoff	0	▽					▦ ▦ ▦ ▦ ⌐		

Studio Vision: Record/playback controls

Without exploring all the boxes, I used the familiar controls to start recording. The Countoff feature at the bottom could have been used to give me an audible cue-in at a chosen tempo.

After recording, I was asked to choose *another* file name. I found this annoying at first until I discovered from the manual that all files have this dual form. The reason is at the heart of computer recording. The second file is used to contain instructions for playing the original recording. Thus if I subsequently edit out a small section, instructions or *pointers* are saved in the second file, telling it to skip over on playback the part that I want to eliminate. This is done without any alteration of the original recording, and is obviously quicker and safer than saving a new file each time an alteration is made. It also enables the Undo feature to be very simple, since all that is undone is the relevant pointer or pointers. This being so, I would have been happier if it had been possible to undo more than one item. For instance, if you select a piece of the audio track and cut a piece out, you then have to move the two pieces together. After you have done the move you can undo it, but not the cut that preceded it. You can always revert to your last saved version, however, since nothing destructive happened to the recording itself.

Working with the Sanz recording, I found that it was comparatively easy to identify unwanted string squeaks or scrapes and to cut them out accurately enough to be imperceptible on the playback. Here is an example:

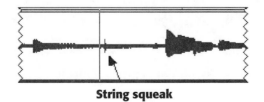

String squeak

To the left of the unwanted squeak may be seen the vertical cursor, which travels along the line of the audio wave during playback. This makes it easy to spot where the imperfections lie. Editing is also simple. After stopping the playback, a click near the unwanted part will produce a vertical cursor that may be dragged over the offending area to select it. Then the selected part may be cleared with a choice from the Edit menu.

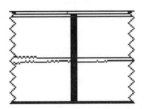

The unwanted area selected by dragging the cursor

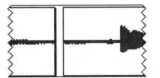

Choose Clear **and the unwanted area is gone**

There is now a gap where the squeak was, and this would produce an audible hiccup when played back. In this case the gap is small enough that it may be eliminated by dragging the right-hand block to the left until the two blocks join. The time lost is not noticeable, but an unattractive sound has disappeared.

The Weird and Wonderful

In addition to these conventional facilities, Studio Vision has some surprising abilities when compared to analog tape editing. For instance, the pitch can be changed without altering the tempo, or the tempo without altering the pitch. In addition, a MIDI track can be made from an audio track, though this is limited to a single musical line and thus of little use in guitar music. However, a guitarist could enter single lines to create a bass part or flute obbligato to add to his audio performance, and audio and MIDI could subsequently be mixed for the final recording. Even more surprising perhaps, an audio track can be converted to MIDI, edited, and then returned to audio. Unfortunately, the single-line restriction applies here as well, so the actual utility is limited.

UPPER-LEVEL PC

New MIDI sequencers pack digital audio capabilities to let you work with sound and music. For the PC two programs, from Cakewalk Music Software and Musicator, let you record, create, and edit MIDI music and wave files in a single integrated environment. These products are ideal if you need to pull a variety of MIDI and wave files or record and balance several tracks of vocals synchronized with your MIDI music tracks. Recording and mixing at this level of sophistication, however, is beyond the province of this book. Some of the more straightforward uses of Cakewalk Pro are discussed below.

CAKEWALK PRO AUDIO

Twelve Tone Systems, Inc.
P.O. Box 760
Watertown, Massachusetts 02272

Cakewalk Pro Audio works well with the SoundBlaster card to enable direct recording. After enabling the microphone in the Creative Mixer I brought up a window that shows audio levels and was able to test that the microphone was working, Then, using the simple controls at the top of the screen, I was able to record once more.

There is a convenient and easily usable window for audio editing, and my first version of the Gaspar Sanz looked like this:

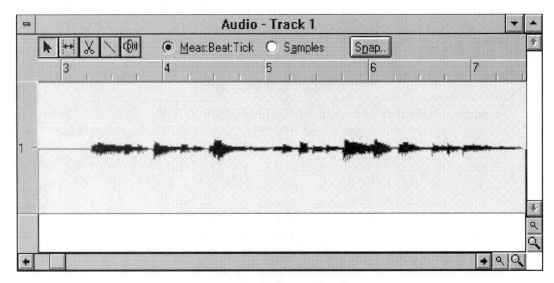

Cakewalk Professional Audio

The volume was somewhat anemic, so I used the convenient feature found in the better audio editors—the **Normalize** command. This increases the sound peaks to a maximum practical level, which compensates for too small a microphone input.

The audio track after normalization

The result now looks and sounds more robust. The change from black to white shows that the audio track has been chosen for editing, done by selecting the arrow cursor from the panel at the top left. The other controls in that panel enabled selection of a chunk of audio for cutting, pasting, or processing, a pair of scissors to make a cut point to isolate one section from another, a line used to create crescendos and diminuendos, and finally the speaker icon, which invokes the *scrub mode*. Scrubbing means dragging a cursor along the audio track so as to hear the sound of each segment. It is a handy way to find and isolate small imperfections, much like the old method of passing a section of tape back and forth over a playback head to find an exact spot.

As before, I was able to spot a string noise in the audio stream, shown below as the bump to the right of the vertical cursor. In this view the track has been spread lengthwise to show more detail, and what is shown is mainly the low level background noise. With the scrub audio facility it was simple to find the exact in and out points and to select the area for deletion.

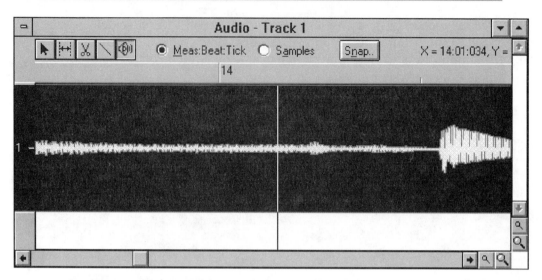

Cakewalk Professional: Locating string noise

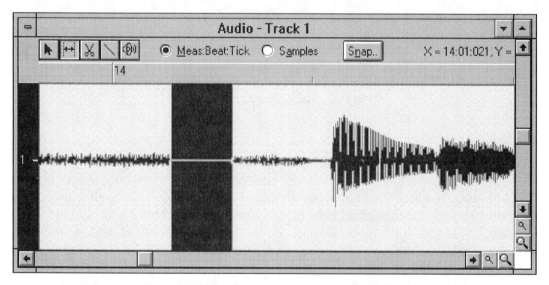

Cakewalk Professional: The noise is eliminated, but a silent spot remains

After the deletion it is necessary, as before, to eliminate the silent passage. This can be done by dragging the right section over to the left, or alternatively a small piece of background noise from either side could be copied and pasted into the flat area. Of these options the dragging is the simpler, since every cut and paste potentially introduces a fractional change of sound if not done perfectly.

This program, like the others mentioned, includes the ability to

70

reverse part of the audio—a rather rare need, I would think, unless you are decoding satanic messages. On a more practical front, there is a ten-octave graphic equalizer for a wide range of tone adjustment. High pass, low pass, band pass, and band stop filters are also available.

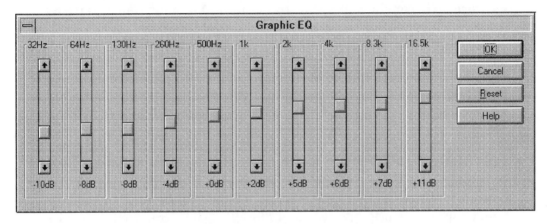

Cakewalk Professional: Graphic equalizer

In addition to the recording programs I've described in this chapter, Musicator (PC only) provides a wide range of features and a musician's (rather than programmer's) approach. Also, the fine Cubase series (Mac, PC) from Steinberg is used in many professional studios.

Home recording to a disk drive is possible for the amateur, particularly if the object is to use it simply as a practice aid and to have a general check on how well a piece is prepared. It could be used to record the other half of a duet, and when used this way the virtually instant rewind can be a distinct asset. For study purposes some people like to play along with an existing record, and all the programs discussed make it possible to record from a track on a CD. Such a recording can then be slowed down in tempo by the high-end programs without changing the pitch, enabling slow practice that could be gradually increased in tempo. Of course, the same thing can be done by making a MIDI version, where tempo changes are instantaneous and simple to do in all programs. The only problem is the labor involved in entering the MIDI from the sheet music, and this is why some companies, such as MIDI Classics (**http://www.infohaus.com/access/by-seller/MIDI_Classics**) sell tracks that contain MIDI versions of classic material.

For professional recording the situation is a bit different. Years ago, when I was considering buying a professional-quality tape recorder, I was lectured by a well-known music publisher on some of the realities. First, he said, I had access to first-class studios that had made major investments in top-rate equipment. These studios would also have an experienced engineer who could decide on the best microphones for the particular situation and would have editing skills acquired through much experience. As far as expense was concerned, the hourly rate, though high, could be kept to a minimum by really good advance preparation of the music to be recorded. His conclusion: spend the time on your instrument and let really expert people take care of your recording needs.

I believed him then, and I still have the same opinion today. If I were making an informal recording to send to friends at Christmas or some similar project, I could imagine recording to disk if I had no other equipment (such as a dedicated digital recorder or high-quality tape recorder). As far as editing is concerned, my experiments led me to believe that it is not quite as simple as the instruction manuals would imply. The range of tonal equalization available with digital recordings seems far more limited compared to the analog equivalent in any but the best (and most expensive) equipment. Perhaps the best feature is the ability to clean up unwanted noises. Some of the features in some of the programs simply didn't appear to work, however, and those that did work needed practice and subsequent tweaking to get them right. The ear is sensitive to the smallest imperfection, and it is easy to leave behind a trace of what you have been editing. Pitch changes sometimes introduce unwanted sounds (known as *chipmunking*), although the high-end programs work hard to overcome these problems. This is a world of high technology, recommended only to those with a strong technical bent.

FIVE
OPTICAL CHARACTER RECOGNITION

O ptical Character Recognition, usually abbreviated to OCR, involves recognizing the contents of a printed page and converting it into a computer file for the purpose of editing or storage.

When dealing with text, the most common usage, the page to be recognized is fed to a conventional optical scanner of the type used to scan and edit photographs and graphics. The resulting scan, which is now a collection of dots simulating the appearance of the original page, is processed by software that examines the contents, recognizes characters, and converts these to the ASCII code used in computers to store text in a compact way. This text may now be easily edited in a word processor and archived economically on disk. Of course editing takes time, and a poor job of recognition can result in more time spent making corrections than would be given to rekeying. For this reason many in the publishing industry are cautious about using OCR until a higher level of accuracy can be achieved.

Applying OCR technology to printed music opens up many exciting possibilities, including the following:

1. Creation of a MIDI file from the printed page so as to have an audible representation of the music. For many guitarists this would be a way to get a quick impression of a complex piece, perhaps more easily than sight-reading it.
2. The scanning of a vocal or duet part for play-along practice.
3. Assistance in the creation by publishers of computer music archives from existing sheet music. Once in the computer, this music can be transmitted by modem to music stores or directly to the user.
4. Assistance in the reengraving of music that is in poor condition so as to produce clean new editions.

Of course, the value of OCR programs is directly related to the time it takes to produce the desired result. This means that the recognition must be good, with a high proportion of music characters recognized correctly prior to editing. Moreover, editing must be achievable simply and quickly. I've examined the two OCR programs discussed in this chapter with these criteria in mind.

NOTESCAN

Temporal Acuity Products
300 120th Ave. NE, Bldg. 1
Bellview, Washington 98005

Manufacturer's description:

"NoteScan Music Scanning Software is an exciting new music scanning utility which brings enhanced power to Nightingale Notation/Composition/Engraving Software. NoteScan is the first computer program which uses Optical Music Character Recognition to read a printed sheet of music directly into a music notation program. This allows the scanned score to be edited, played back, transposed, rearranged, and republished, all within the single environment of the Nightingale music notation application.

NoteScan is a completely new approach to the concept of scanning music. Early introductions of music scanning software yielded only a string of MIDI data, which first had to be edited for mistakes, and then imported into a MIDI/Music application for further and often extensive work to produce a finished score. Because of the built-in power, ease of use, and sophistication of Nightingale, TAP has chosen to have NoteScan import scanned music files directly into Nightingale, without the user doing any prior editing. This eliminates one entire level of editing tasks, saving time and effort for the user."

Taking our standard test piece, "Adelita," I first experimented with the NoteScan system, developed by Cindy Grande and packaged with the Nightingale program. There is an obvious convenience to linking a scan into a program that you already use for other purposes, since its familiarity will speed up the editing process.

I begin by placing the music on my flat-bed scanner and setting the resolution as required in the NoteScan manual to 200 dots per inch (dpi). I then save the scan in TIFF format and am now ready to have it processed by NoteScan. TIFF, or Tag Image File Format, developed by Adobe Systems, is a popular means of saving graphics files. It has the advantage of being interchangeable between Macintosh and PC computers.

After running NoteScan I load my scanned picture. A dialog box gives me the opportunity to let NoteScan interpret the key and time signatures or to override these. I decide to let NoteScan do its best. Then the software commences its task of recognizing notes and symbols. On the screen I can see this work in progress, since part of each element that is recognized goes into reverse video (white on black).

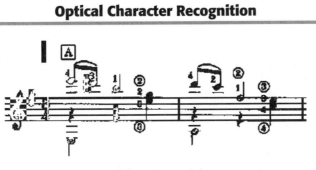

NoteScan at work

The illustration above, taken from the NoteScan screen, shows the original graphic scan of the first two measures of "Adelita." At this point NoteScan has recognized the clef and time signature and has started on the notes. After about three minutes, during which the screen changes to show the part of the page being scanned, a message appears to say that recognition of the sixteen measures is complete.

Now the resulting interpretation has to be loaded into Nightingale. After starting this program I choose **Load NoteScan File** from the File menu and choose my new file from the selection box that appears. At this point I get a warning from Nightingale:

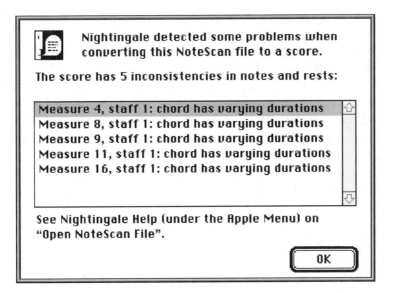

NoteScan: Checking problems

I decide to ignore these for now and click on OK. Now I am presented with the first interpretation:

An unedited interpretation from NoteScan

The first thing I notice is that the quarter rest on the first beat in the middle voice has been replaced (and offset to the left) by a thirty-second rest and a bar line, so I start by eliminating those. This is as simple as selecting them and hitting the delete key. Next I want to change the time signature, so I bring the main control palette into view by choosing it from the View menu. I also choose to work on a single voice for corrections, which seems to be a necessary procedure, so I choose this also from the View menu.

At this point I remove the remaining quarter rest, since for simplicity I have decided to accept down to two voices. A voice can have a chord in it as long as the notes of the chord all have the same time value. Next I select and beam the upper eighth notes, which for some reason makes them change stem direction. I correct this, and at this point select the whole piece and choose **Multi-Voice Notation** from the Notes and Rests menu. Now it becomes easy to beam the whole piece correctly with a general beaming command.

Retracing my every step in correcting the score would give a false impression of a tremendous labor. There was a fair amount to be done, however, and a good familiarity with the Nightingale editing capabilities is a necessity. The score chosen was a hard test in that it had many extra signs for fingering, strings, and so on, which had to be ignored by the software in its search for essentials. Once the editing was done I was able to play the piece directly through Nightingale's MIDI playback.

NoteScan exists currently for the Macintosh. For the PC the leading, and almost only, program is MIDISCAN, from Musitek, developed by Chris Newell.

MIDISCAN

Musitek
410 Bryant Circle
Ojai, California 93023

Manufacturer's description:

"MIDISCAN for Windows, Version 2.5 MIDISCAN converts printed sheet music into multitrack MIDI files. MIDISCAN processes virtually any type of score up to 24

pages at a time. Note and rest durations, note pitches, chords, ties, accidentals, bar-lines, clefs, key and time signatures are all recognized with 90–98% accuracy. MIDISCAN is TWAIN compatible and works with all MIDI sequencing and notation software. An easy-to-use editing environment makes cleanup of the reconstructed file quick and intuitive. Processing time takes from 30 seconds per page (Pentium 100) to 3 minutes per page (386 SX). Now, MIDISCAN v2.5 supports the revolutionary new music notation file format, NIFF (Notation Interchange File Format)."

With MIDISCAN I applied the same test piece as with NoteScan, with the difference that it was scanned at a higher definition (300 dpi), as recommended by the manufacturer.

MIDISCAN has a slightly different approach to the correction process. After the music has been scanned and a TIFF format image prepared, these pages are imported into MIDISCAN for the initial recognition process. At this point the user is able to select multiple pages for recognition and also to widen or narrow the recognition area for each staff according to the appearance of the original. This accommodates staves with extremes of leger lines above or below that would escape the standard recognition area. Systems with multiple staves are accommodated, even those that increase or decrease in size from page to page.

As with NoteScan there is a visual presentation while the recognition is in process, and the user can see both staves and notes as they are processed.

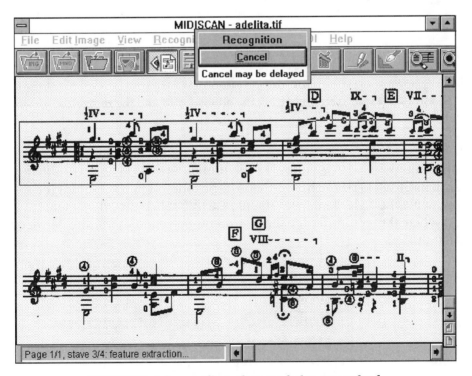

MIDISCAN: A box outlines the area being recognized

Here the similarity with NoteScan ends, because MIDISCAN creates an interim file for correction purposes prior to the creation of the MIDI playback version. This is presented on a split screen for comparison against the original scan.

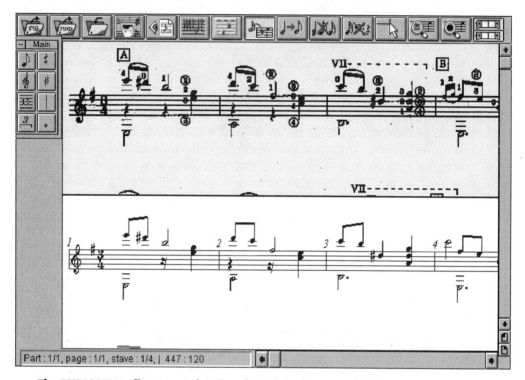

The MIDISCAN split screen, showing the original scan and the recognized version

The split screen is a great convenience and speeds up the inevitable correction process. The controls for editing are well organized so that the left hand uses keys to change major functions, such as inserting or erasing, while the right hand uses the mouse to finalize the adjustments.

When the editing is finished, a menu selection starts the MIDI creation process.

The MIDI file menu

The MIDI file may then be played back through the built-in sequencer. The edited file may also be printed.

Musitek: MIDI sequencer

OCR: THE BOTTOM LINE

It would be hard to say at this point in the development of music character recognition that much time is saved in making a MIDI version of a given piece of printed music. The total process from scan to edited final version is probably comparable to entering the music with a MIDI keyboard because small errors creep in and sometimes are not apparent until the MIDI version is played back. Then the whole editing process must be resumed and the MIDI tested again. A skilled operator will acquire editing facility to shorten the time taken, but the same is true of any entry method.

Perhaps the strongest argument for OCR is that for the person lacking in keyboard skills and daunted by manual entry, the scanning and editing are less mentally taxing and hence less laborious. As with many tedious operations, using the computer can make the work more fun, which is a justification even if no time is really gained.

Chris Newell, the developer of MIDISCAN, and Cindy Grande, the developer of NoteScan, are both working with the support of other manufacturers to produce a standard music file format so that music files with full graphic information can be interchangeable between different programs. Cindy is the technical coordinator for the project, which is known as the Notation Interchange File Format (NIFF).

SIX
MUSIC STUDY WITH A COMPUTER

In general, it is hard to conceive of better music instruction than that given by a live teacher on a one-to-one basis. This is a luxury not available to all students, however, and lesser methods of instruction are preferable to no instruction at all. As one who has been involved in teaching by means of books and television, I am well aware of the strengths and limitations of both. Nevertheless, the heartwarming response of students who are geographically isolated or lacking funds for private lessons makes it clear that teaching aids of any kind are most welcome.

The strength of the computer is that it can make a game out of memorization and drill that would otherwise be laborious. Self-taught musicians usually avoid boring tasks, for the very good reason that they chose music for pleasure and entertainment. But certain essentials speed up the road to success, not the least of which is learning the guitar fingerboard. It is unfortunate that whereas piano students learn where the notes are almost at the first lesson, guitarists can go for months or even years with only a vague knowledge of the higher frets. History tells us that publishers of guitar music have found the major demand to be for "easy" music, and this means music in the lower positions of the guitar. Easy music in higher positions is considered difficult simply because many amateurs have not learned the fingerboard.

A number of instructional programs are available as CD-ROMs, and these are dealt with below. At this point it is a good moment to mention an exceptionally well-thought-out music theory course available on floppy disks for Macintosh. The creation of the music teacher Jeffrey Evans and a winner of many awards, this moderate-priced program is known as Practica Musica.

PRACTICA MUSICA

Ars Nova
P. O. Box 637
Kirkland, Washington 98083

Manufacturer's Description:

"Practica Musica 3, the most complete music theory and ear training package available for the Macintosh, contains 16 exercises, including Pitch Matching, Pitch Reading, Rhythm Matching, Rhythm Reading, Scales/Key Signatures, Interval Playing, Interval Spelling, Interval Ear Training, Chord Playing, Chord Spelling, Chord Ear Training, Chord Progression Ear Training, Pitch Dictation, Rhythm Dictation, Pitch & Rhythm Dictation, and Melody Writing/Listening. Each exercise has four levels of difficulty, making it suitable for both beginning and advanced musicians. Additionally, while Practica Musica 3 is fully MIDI compatible, MIDI is not required.

A convenient onscreen keyboard (or new fretboard for guitar users!) may be used for note entry.

Sampled sounds, available when using the built-in Macintosh speaker, include piano, guitar, pipe organ, and voice.

Most other music training software reads lists of premade exercises, but Practica Musica can do more than read its library of tunes; it can compose endless numbers of new melodies, rhythms, and chord progressions for you to practice with—they will always be fresh. It listens to your responses and replies with appropriate correction when needed.

Practica Musica is designed to be easy to use for anyone interested in music, from high school students to music majors. It is installed at hundreds of university campuses, conservatories, and high schools across the United States, Canada, the United Kingdom, and Australia, and is used at home all around the globe."

Practica Musica comes with an operating manual and the book *Windows on Music*. This text, when used in conjunction with the program, provides an introduction to music theory including scales, pitch and rhythm notation, chord formation and progressions, and elements of form, voice leading, and melody building. These topics, which can seem intimidating to the beginning guitarist, are presented with great clarity and are supported at every stage with "activities." These activities take the place of written exercises, and the interactivity with the computer means that errors can be pointed out and scores kept of achievement. The computer's messages and reactions are kindly and encouraging, and mistakes are not greeted with rude sounds or derision. Several students may use the program and have their individual scores kept.

PRACTICA

MVSICA™

©1987-1994 Jeffrey Evans
All rights reserved.

ARS NOVA
- Please click to continue -

W.A.Mozart

First use: Minutes logged: Last use:
11/22/96   0   11/22/96

▮▮ = mastery attained	Level 1	Level 2	Level 3	Level 4
Pitch matching				
Pitch reading				
Rhythm matching				
Rhythm reading				
Pitch/Rhythm reading				
Scales				
Interval playing				
Interval spelling				
Interval ear training				
Chord playing				
Chord spelling				
Chord ear training				
Chord progression ear training				
Pitch dictation, library				
Pitch dictation, generated				
Rhythm dictation, library				
Rhythm dictation, generated				
Full dictation, library				
Full dictation, generated				

Practica Musica: Startup screen

WORKING WITH PRACTICA MUSICA

Two of the simplest activities in this program are of great use to the beginning guitar student. When the program is first opened, the default starting point is headed "Experiment with Pitch." The opening screen shows a piano keyboard, but this can easily be changed to the guitar equivalent by a choice from the Options menu. A choice of the correct clef, a click on the small guitar icon to the right under the word MIDI, and a click on the loudspeaker icon to the left, and the user is ready to experiment with relating the notes on the guitar to their pitch and appearance on the musical staff.

Using this setup the student can click on any part of the fingerboard and hear the note played. Here the A at the fifth fret has been selected. At the same time the appropriate note is shown on the small staff.

Similar simple experimentation can be done with chords (up to four notes)—when the notes are selected by clicking on the fingerboard the program identifies and displays the correct name for the chord.

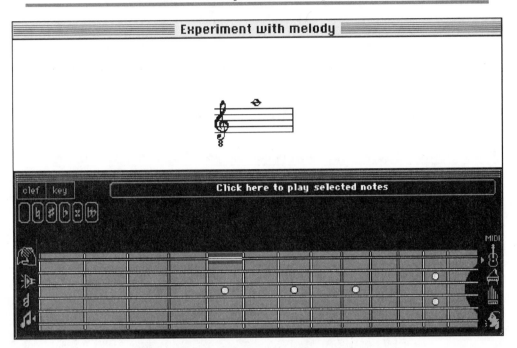

Practica Musica: Learning the guitar fingerboard

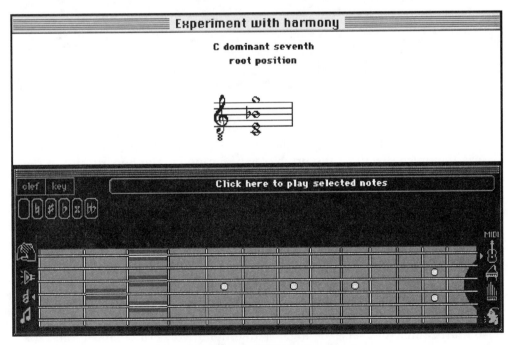

Practica Musica: Discovering chords

After some basic memorization and experimentation it is time to choose "Pitch Reading" from the Activities menu. Now melodies will appear in staff notation for the student to match by playing the appropriate note. For the guitarist this is done by clicking with the mouse on each fret in turn to match the notes on the staff, and at the end both accuracy and speed are measured and stored in the student's record.

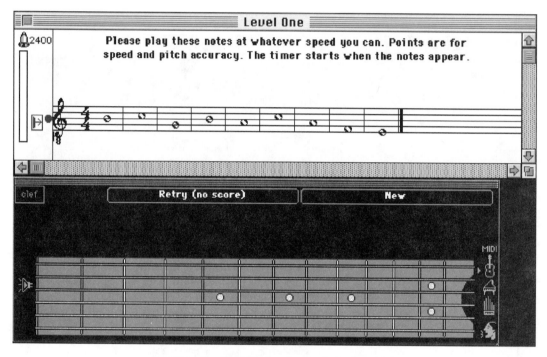

Practica Musica: Playing an assigned melody

Practica Musica is not designed exclusively for the guitar, but neither was the musical staff or the principles of harmony. The opportunity to see harmonic patterns and so on in either keyboard or guitar format can greatly aid the student's understanding of chord formation and progression.

As the lessons progress, simple dictation is introduced. A brief melody is chosen from a menu, and after it is played, the student then tries to write or play it from memory.

In the example on page 85 the rhythm is given above the notes to be entered. Later exercises require that both rhythm and pitch be entered.

An interesting feature is that the program will generate random melodies for this dictation activity. The random melodies are much harder to grasp, since they lack the logic of traditional Western compositions. For the more advanced student they can present a real challenge.

It is possible to explore only the simplest aspects here, but it should

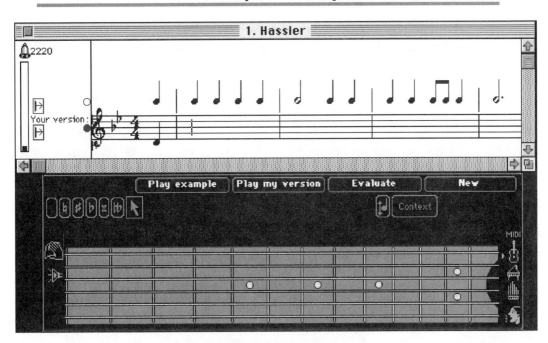

Practica Musica: Simple dictation

be stressed that a tremendous wealth of activities moves progressively higher in level, with some worthy challenges to any musician.

Further interactivity is possible using Autoscore, offered for a modest price to users of Practica Musica. This program enables students to sing into a microphone connected to the computer and have the pitch recognized—a great assistance to the eventual mastery of sight-singing.

The program also deals with tuning and temperament, with the opportunity to hear the difference between, for instance, equal and meantone temperaments. The acoustics of music are discussed, as are the physics behind instrumental timbre. But the most outstanding advantage of this package is the clear, nonacademic explanation of the fundamentals of music theory with the accompanying activities that help to fix the principles in the mind. This program is a shining example of what can be done with a program that is well thought out and skillfully constructed.

CD-ROM MUSIC RESOURCES

As explained above, the CD-ROM is so named because it is a compact disk that stores *read only memory*. It differs from a conventional CD in being able to present pictures and text as well as sound when played on a CD-ROM player. The amount of available storage is large (700 Mb), comparable to a good-sized hard drive, and the interactive nature of the medium makes it particularly useful for reference, education, and games.

The word *interactive* can mean many things. At its simplest it compares to choosing a band on a conventional CD with a remote control—the user simply selects from many choices an area of interest, which is then presented as rapidly as the particular program permits. For instance, an encyclopedia topic may be selected from a menu or with a search device that invites the user to type in a search word or phrase. The response may take a few seconds while the mechanism finds the appropriate place on the disk and brings the required information to the screen. CD-ROMs do not access material as quickly as hard drives, and if the information to be found involves color pictures or movies, the delay is greater still. This is perhaps the biggest reason that the medium has not realized its potential.

CD-ROM drives are almost the norm in new computers, and often a variety of disks are offered free as an inducement to the buyer. In many cases, however, interest fades after some desultory exploration of the free items, and the drive is subsequently rarely used.

Without a strong market for new disks, the funds cease to be available for the production of new items; because rather considerable funds are needed for imaginative production, the whole field has tended to narrow down rather than expand. Nevertheless, there are some items of interest in the area of music history, and also an intriguing source of public domain sheet music. The Voyager company in particular has produced some music history and analysis titles that will be of general interest to music students.

VOYAGER

514 Market Loop, Suite 104
West Dundee, Illinois 60118

Voyager was founded in 1985, a joint venture of Janus Films and Voyager Press. Taking its name from the exploratory spacecraft, Voyager released laser discs of contemporary and classic films in an effort that would become the Criterion Collection. When, in 1987, it first became possible to control a laser disc player from a Macintosh with Hypercard, the company released its first computer-controlled interactive discs. The Hypercard program provides the facility to access different parts of the CD-ROM and to play the musical examples by a simple system of buttons.

Beethoven's Ninth Symphony

Considered to be the first consumer CD-ROM (it was released in 1988), the first entry in the outstanding CD Companion series from Voyager is built around a performance of Beethoven's Ninth Symphony by the

Vienna Philharmonic and the Vienna State Opera Chorus. Robert Winter, a classical pianist and music professor at the University of California at Los Angeles, provides a commentary that clearly and elegantly illuminates this complex orchestral work.

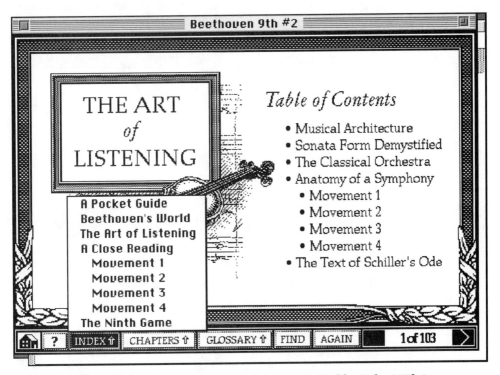

Voyager: Beethoven's Ninth Symphony, presented by Robert Winter

The Index provides a pop-up menu for simple selection of the major topics. In the above example the Art of Listening has been chosen.

Clicking on any text in the Table of Contents will jump forward to the appropriate chapter. Otherwise, the individual pages may be taken in sequence by clicking on the arrow in the bottom right corner of the screen.

Winter gives a detailed and thorough analysis of the work, and the individual themes may be both heard and seen in musical notation. As the music progresses in the Close Reading segment, explanations appear in the left window detailing themes, mood, instrumentation, and so on. A long essay, "Beethoven's World," combines an absorbing biography and a bibliography. A particularly interesting chapter quotes extracts from the composer's "conversation books," in which visitors wrote down what they were saying to Beethoven in his later years of deafness. We learn that at the first performance of the symphony, a fifth round of applause was interrupted by a demand for quiet by the chief of police.

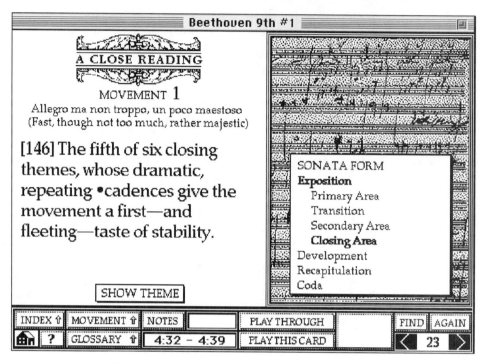

Voyager: Descriptive analysis as the music plays

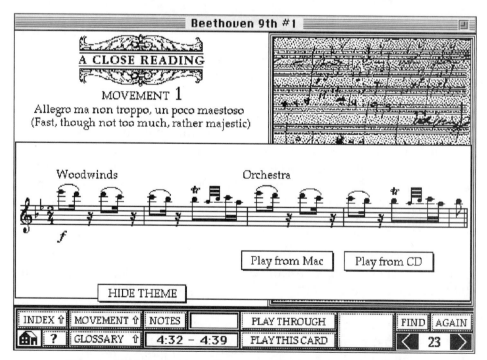

Voyager: Clicking on Show Theme **reveals the notation examples.**

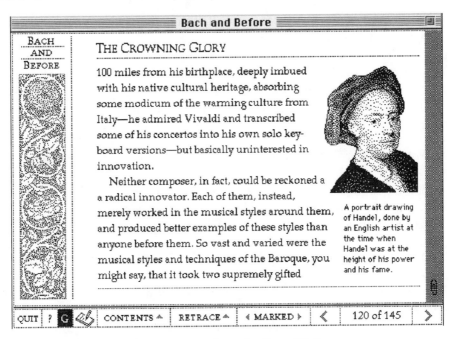

Voyager: A page from *Bach and Before*

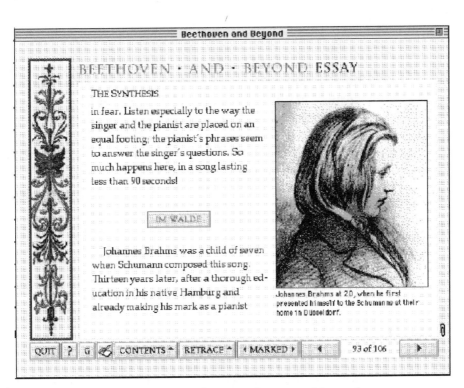

Voyager: A page from *Beethoven and Beyond*

At the end of the CD-ROM a detailed and interesting game tests your knowledge of the work.

Also from Robert Winter is *The "Dissonant" Quartet: An Interactive Companion to Mozart's String Quartet in C Major, K465*. This follows the same pattern of thorough but easily understood analysis.

Other CD Companions for Macintosh with similar detailed analysis include:

Antonin Dvořák's Symphony No. 9, *From the New World* (Robert Winter)

Franz Schubert: The "Trout" Quintet (Alan Rich)

Richard Strauss: Three Tone Poems (Russell Steinberg)

Igor Stravinsky: *The Rite of Spring* (Robert Winter)

From the same publisher comes the "So I've Heard" Series, a splendid historical series selected and annotated by the author and critic Alan Rich. Here essays and notes accompany extracts rather than complete works, selected by a seasoned listener of excellent taste. These extracts come from a wide variety of sources, and full details are given, including record company and reference numbers for the many who will want to collect the complete recordings. The overall superb recording quality adds even further to the pleasure.

In the first volume, *Bach and Before*, the graphics are in black and white, which means they will appear essentially the same on all screens. Color would add beauty to the presentation but has very little real importance, since the tasteful engravings, originally black and white, add decoration without stealing attention from the essential musical content. Later volumes have color in the pages and decorations but essentially keep to monochrome graphics.

Alan Rich's presentations offer extensive essays interspersed with the musical examples. These examples can be played by clicking on the buttons that appear throughout the text, as in the *Beethoven and Beyond* example on page 89.

ENHANCED CD

INTERSOUND

Intersound
11810 Wills Road
Rothwell, Georgia 30077

The term *enhanced CD* describes an audio CD that includes additional multimedia features. It differs from those previously described in that it can be played on a CD player as a conventional audio CD if a person wishes to disregard the additional features.

Intersound Inc. has a music history series of this type, playable on both Macintosh and PC computers. The level of information presented is aimed at the young or uninformed audience, but the presentation is lavish, with full color graphics. The various choices include small essays being read over looped background music. The graphics change with the topics, but the music plays on. In the case of the Baroque volume, the background music is a sort of "switched on" version of Pachelbel's omnipresent canon with synthesizer and snare drums. This is not a part of the audio CD, however, which has the canon in conventional form.

Intersound: The CD-ROM choices

A consistent format is followed throughout the Intersound music history offerings. Notation, a segment common to all of them, gives a brief explanation of note values and the basics of notation. Similarly, Meet the Orchestra gives explanations about the various instrumental divisions of the orchestra. Unfortunately, this is over a background score; illustrations of the sound of the individual instruments would have been more useful. Keeping Score shows a sample score for the student to follow, and Listening Post shows the full musical program with the selections playable by clicking on the title.

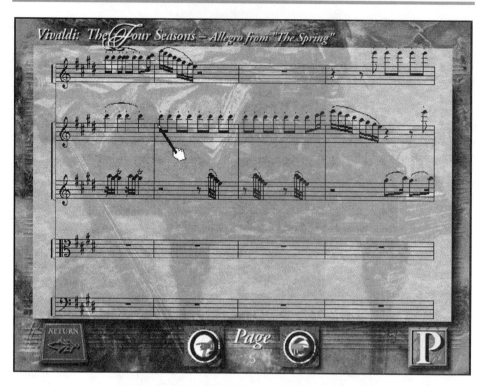

Intersound: A score for the student to follow

The final selection, A Musical Journey, runs the essay with graphic illustrations more or less appropriate to the text.

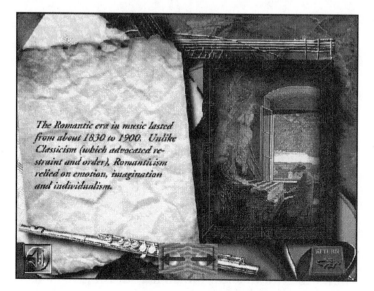

Intersound: Introduction to *The Romantic Era*

ZANE PUBLISHING INC.

Zane also has a music history series aimed at the ten years to adult group. Their presentations make full use of the multimedia environment. For instance, the *Romanticism to Contemporary* volume from the Music History series contains an eighty-nine-minute multimedia presentation and includes 850 images, with excerpts from works by fifteen major composers from Beethoven to Gershwin. One hundred questions are included for self-testing. These start very simply, with such questions as "Niccolò Paganini, the great Romantic virtuoso, was renowned for playing what musical instrument?" or "Who composed the popular oratorio *Messiah*?," and range to modestly greater difficulty.

Titles
Through the Classical Period
Romanticism to Contemporary
Music and Culture
The Art of Listening
American Folk Music
History of Jazz

With CD-ROM, as with all media, it is the content that counts. The colorizing of old films was considered by many to be unnecessary and in fact annoyed many viewers familiar with the original movies. Yet color is considered an important feature of multimedia presentations. What is in fact really important in addition to the content is its accessibility. People hate to wait while items slowly load, or when it is impossible to access directly part of a program without returning to former menus that may operate slowly or have irritating background music. We are used to television sets that change channels or switch off instantly. Yet some CD-ROMs are hard to escape from without navigation and hard to restart without slow loading. The venerable Hypercard program on which the Voyager programs are based still holds up well in the face of jazzier presentations, though one could wish for a Quit button to replace the Home symbol that throws you into a seemingly inescapable "Welcome to Hypercard" environment.

Entertainment and educational CD-ROMs will undoubtedly survive and improve, and will perhaps become commercially viable if a more satisfactory system of retailing them emerges.

Apart from entertainment, the CD-ROM format is becoming the normal distribution means for large conventional programs that would otherwise require a multitude of floppy disks. For this reason alone a CD-ROM drive should be included in your computer. In addition, as devices to record to CD become less expensive, the high capacity makes the CD an attractive medium for backing up large amounts of data, since the laser disk is in general more stable than magnetic media. At the present state of the art, such recording devices do not operate at a high enough data transfer speed to be suitable for audio recording. However, recorded takes from a conventional hard drive could be transferred and stored this way.

SEVEN

CONNECTING WITH
THE WORLD

MODEMS

The fundamental tool for connecting your computer with the larger computer world is the *modem*—a device that sends and receives information via conventional telephone lines. Modems may be internal—computers are often shipped with them already installed—or may be a stand-alone unit that plugs into the back of the computer. On the PC, modems are more usually internal, and modem cards may be bought for installation in a spare slot.

Modems have a speed rating to show how fast they can transfer information to and from your telephone. Because modern networks tend to use color graphics, and these take time to load, the speed of your modem can make a big difference. Modem makers have been pushing up the speed over the years until now the limitation is not so much the modem as the quality of the telephone line. Currently the top speed (baud rate) for ordinary lines is 33.2 Kbs (kilobits per second), just a neck ahead of the 28.8 Kbs previously considered the highest speed that an ordinary phone line could handle. In reality, unless you have a perfect line the 33.2 Kbs modem will probably drop back to 28.8 or less, and most on-line services are currently limited to a top rate of 28.8. If you are buying a new modem, consider that 28.8 Kbs would probably serve most needs, but the 33.2 would put you on the current cutting edge. The previous top rate is always cheaper that the latest, since manufacturers have old stock to unload. Currently you can buy a 14.4 Kbs modem for less than half the price of a 28.8, but you will get half the performance and probably regret it. The difference between 33.2 and 28.8 is less significant for the reasons mentioned above.

As well as taking data from the computer and feeding it to the telephone line, modems compress the data to give an apparently greater speed, or *throughput,* as it is called. At the other end, the receiving modem does the same thing in reverse, decompressing what is coming in. For this to work, both modems must talk the same language, or *protocol;* fortunately, such systems are becoming standardized, so the average

95

buyer does not have to research this when buying a new modem. At this time the V.34 compression system is in common use, and it would be a mistake to buy a modem without this feature.

Just one more technical point. When modems talk to each other they need to establish at the beginning what they have in common. For instance a 14.4 Kbs modem communicating with a 28.8 must establish the fact that 14.4 Kbs will be the fastest possible speed. To help in this situation, modems send a *handshaking message*—a coded series of letters and numbers that helps the negotiation along. In addition, the modem can be set by the user to invoke certain preferences that may be requested by a particular service that you are using. Normally a modem will have a basic default setting, or *initialization string*, that is set by the factory and that will work in most cases.

USING THE COMMUNICATIONS PROGRAM

Modems are normally sold with two software programs, a communications program and a fax program, the latter because many people use their modems to send faxes. The communications program is a wonderful tool and the main one in use before on-line services became so popular. As an example, the communications program supplied with my PC modem card is called BitCom, a component of BitWare Plus, available from Computer Associates International Inc., Islandia, New York (800-243-9462). Starting it up shows this screen:

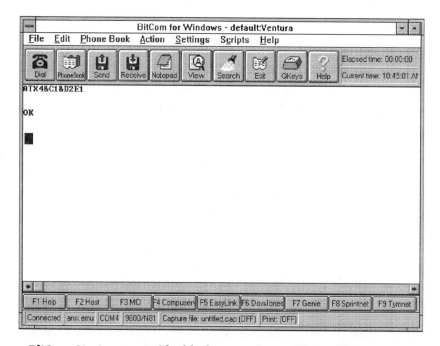

BitCom: Startup screen (the black square is actually a winking cursor)

Virtually all modems respond to commands established by the Hayes modem manufacturers, and usually the words "Hayes compatible" will appear somewhere on the modem package. This means that a series of standardized commands may be used, starting usually with the letters *AT*. In the startup page above, the modem has automatically sent the command for its initialization string and displays **OK** on the screen to confirm that all is in order. At the point where the cursor is winking I may type the command **ATDT,** meaning Dial Touchtone, followed by the number I want to dial. The modem will automatically dial the number, and if all is well a "connect" message will appear on the screen.

If my object was simply to link up with a friend, perhaps to send or receive some files, I would have warned him in advance to set his program up to be ready to receive. If he had a similar setup to mine he would choose **Auto Answer** from the Action drop-down menu.

BitCom: The Action menu

His computer would respond by confirming to him that he was standing by:

Bitcom: Awaiting a call

When my call was received, his modem would automatically connect and put a message on his screen: **Connect 28800** (or whatever highest

97

speed was common to both our modems). We could then type messages back and forth, which might look something like this:

```
┌─────────────────────────────────────────────────────────────────┐
│ ─        BitCom for Windows - default:Ventura        ▼  ▲         │
├─────────────────────────────────────────────────────────────────┤
│  File   Edit   Phone Book   Action   Settings   Scripts   Help    │
├─────────────────────────────────────────────────────────────────┤
│  ☎     📖     📤     📥     📄     📰     🖌     📝    📀    ?    │ Elapsed time: 00:00:00   │
│ Dial PhoneBook Send  Receive Notepad  View  Search  Edit  QKeys Help │ Current time: 10:18:08 AM │
├─────────────────────────────────────────────────────────────────┤
│ ATX4&C1&D2E1                                                      │
│                                                                   │
│ OK                                                                │
│ CONNECT 28800                                                     │
│ hi John - are you ready for the Carcassi file                     │
│ yes - go ahead                                                    │
│ OK here it comes█                                                 │
│                                                                   │
└─────────────────────────────────────────────────────────────────┘
│ ← │■│                                                          │→ │
├─────────────────────────────────────────────────────────────────┤
│ F1 Help │ F2 Host │ F3 MCI │ F4 Compuserv │ F5 EasyLink │ F6 DowJones │ F7 Genie │ F8 Sprintnet │ F9 Tymnet │
├─────────────────────────────────────────────────────────────────┤
│ Connected │ ansi.emu │ COM4 │ 9600/N81 │ Capture file: untitled.cap (OFF) │ Print: (OFF) │
└─────────────────────────────────────────────────────────────────┘
```

BitCom: Sending a file by modem

My next step would be to choose **Send File** from the Action menu. The program asks me how I want to send the file:

```
┌──────────────────────────────────────┐
│ ─   Send File - Select Protocol       │
├──────────────────────────────────────┤
│ ┌──────────────┐    ┌─────────────┐   │
│ │ ASCII        │    │     OK      │   │
│ │ Xmodem       │    └─────────────┘   │
│ │ Ymodem       │                      │
│ │ Kermit       │    ┌─────────────┐   │
│ │ Zmodem       │    │   Cancel    │   │
│ │              │    └─────────────┘   │
│ │              │                      │
│ │              │    ┌─────────────┐   │
│ │              │    │ Settings... │   │
│ └──────────────┘    └─────────────┘   │
└──────────────────────────────────────┘
```

BitCom: Protocol choice

Zmodem is one of several protocols used in transferring files. It would be nice if all these choices were standardized, but as new and better ways to do things have evolved they have been added to the traditional methods rather than replacing them. Zmodem is fast and efficient, and a good fallback choice if in doubt.

Next a file dialog box appears so I can select the file to send.

BitCom: Choosing a file to send

After making my choice I click on the Send button. At the other end my friend will see a report of progress on his screen. From now on the process is all automatic, and very soon he will have the file saved on his hard drive.

Although this process seems to require quite a few steps, it is very straightforward once it has been done a few times. Unfortunately, there is a tendency to forget the steps if transfers are made only infrequently, so it is a good idea to make a simple chart of the steps. Computers can be infuriatingly unforgiving if something is out of place.

A TRIP TO THE LOCAL LIBRARY

One useful way to try out your modem, and indeed one of the more truly practical uses for a home computer, is to access the catalog of your local library. There are normally no fees for this, and it is extremely handy to be able to check from home whether a book you want is in the system and available.

You will need some basic information from your local library so that you are in tune with its settings. Your librarian can tell you how fast to set your modem and how to set some other options. It may seem complicated, but these choices are presented as simple menu items, and once you have entered the correct settings you will be able to save them and easily invoke the right setup any time in the future. Like many things with the computer, the first time is always the worst, but usually it is worth the initial preparation.

My local library specifies that it prefers a VT100 terminal (another of those annoying choices), operates at 9600 baud, and uses one stop bit and no parity. These items are details of the exchange of communication that you do not need (or probably want) to understand. You can simply pull down menus in your communications program until you find the choices, and then save the settings so you don't have to do this again. Your program will also be able to make some form of address book entry, so that as well as saving these initial choices you may also have the telephone number easily available for automatic dialing.

BitCom: A Phone Book entry

Now you are ready to make the call. In the example above all you would have to do is make the selection (in this case Ventura County Library) and click on the Dial button.

The first screen that comes up will probably welcome you, and possibly check your settings by giving you a test picture with which to make any final adjustments. Again, this is a one-time affair. Then you will probably get a screen like this one from my home library system:

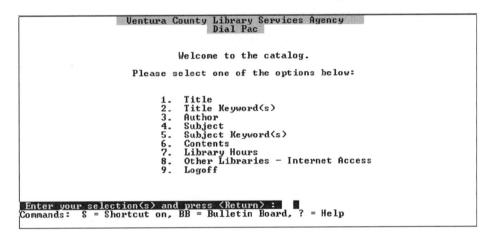

```
        Ventura County Library Services Agency
                      Dial Pac

                Welcome to the catalog.

         Please select one of the options below:

              1.   Title
              2.   Title Keyword(s)
              3.   Author
              4.   Subject
              5.   Subject Keyword(s)
              6.   Contents
              7.   Library Hours
              8.   Other Libraries - Internet Access
              9.   Logoff


 Enter your selection(s) and press <Return> :  ■
Commands:   S = Shortcut on,  BB = Bulletin Board,  ? = Help
```

Ventura County Library: Catalog options

Notice that almost all operations involve typing in a number or letter to make a choice. After the selection is made, the computer's Return key is pressed. Let's make an actual search for guitar-related materials. First we choose the number for a subject search, and this is what arrives:

```
        Ventura County Library Services Agency
                      Dial Pac

 *----------------  SUBJECT AUTHORITY SEARCH EXAMPLE  ---------------*

        Examples:
                    SPACE TRAVEL    (Multiple word subjects)

                    VEGETAB         (Note: OK to shorten subject)



 *--------------------------------------------------------------*

 Enter subject heading :
Commands:   SO = Start Over,  B = Back,  ? = Help
```

Ventura County Library: Subject search examples

We type in the word *guitar,* and here is what we get:

```
                 Ventura County Library Services Agency
                                Dial Pac
Your Search: GUITAR

     Selected (May be truncated)                                    Titles
     1. Guitar -- Group instruction                                    0

     2.    See:  Guitar -- Methods -- Group instruction                1

     3. Guitar -- Handbooks, manuals, etc.                             1

     4. Guitar -- History                                             5

     5. Guitar -- Instruction and study                              15

     6. Guitar -- Maintenance and repair                              4

     7. Guitar -- Methods                                            13

                                  - - - More on Next Screen - - -
 Enter a line number for more detail :
Commands:   SO = Start Over, B = Back, P = Prev Screen, <Return> = Next Screen,
            RS = Review Search, ? = Help
```

Ventura County Library: Guitar

To see if a copy is available of Frederic Grunfeld's excellent anecdotal history of the guitar, I type the number 4 to look at histories. Here is what comes up:

```
                 Ventura County Library Services Agency
                                Dial Pac
Your Search: Guitar -- History

     AUTHOR/TITLE/EDITION                                        CALL NO.
 1.   Wheeler, Tom.                                              R787.612
        American guitars : an illustrated history /

 2.                                                              787.6109
        The Guitar : the history, the music, the players /

 3.   Wheeler, Tom (Thomas Hutchin)                              787.87197
        American guitars : an illustrated history /
        Rev. and updated ed.
 4.   Whitford, Eldon.                                           787.87
        Gibson's fabulous flat-top guitars : an illustrated his

 5.   Grunfeld, Frederic V.                                      787.6109
        The art and times of the guitar : an illustrated histor

 Enter an item number for more detail :
Commands:   SO = Start Over, B = Back, SL = Sort List, RS = Review Search,
   ? = Help
```

Ventura County Library: Looking for guitar histories

I have struck lucky, so I type the number 5 to see if copies are available.

```
         Ventura County Library Services Agency
                        Dial Pac
Author   Grunfeld, Frederic V.
Title    The art and times of the guitar : an ...          Holds:    0

    CALL NUMBER                  STATUS           LIBRARY
  1. NONFICTION - ADULT          checked In       Camarillo
     787.6109
  2. NONFICTION - ADULT          checked In       H.P. Wright
     787.6109




Choose a command :   ▮
Commands:   SO = Start Over,  B = Back,  PH = Place a Hold,  ? = Help
```

Ventura County Library: Checking for availability

Again luck is with me—copies are available in two local libraries. From my computer I have the option of placing a hold on the book, so that it is ready for me when I go to pick it up. Alternatively, I can request my nearest library to have it sent over.

Before we leave the library system, a *gateway* to other library systems and facilities is provided as a public service. This is achieved through the Internet, but all I have to do is make the various selections as they are offered to enter the other systems. Once again, a similar series of screens and choices will appear.

```
         Ventura County Library Services Agency
                        Dial Pac
                                                    11 ITEMS
                 GATEWAY ACCESS                     PAGE 1 OF 1

     1. *LIB.BGOLD  Santa Barbara & San Luis Obispo County Libraries
     2. *LIB.SJVLS  San Joaquin Library System
     3. *LIB.UC.ME  University of California Libraries Catalog
     4. CAL.AGRI    California Markets (ATI-NET)
     5. GOPHER.UCS  Infoslug/UC Santa Cruz Gopher
     6. GOV.FDA     Food and Drug Administration Bulletin Board
     7. GOV.FEDIX   Federal Information Exchange (FEDIX)
     8. GOV.NASA    NASA Space Exploration Database
     9. WEATHER     Weather Underground
    10. WWW.CORNEL  Cornell Legal Information World Wide Web site
    11. WWW.SUNSIT  University of North Carolina World Wide Web site.




Enter a Gate Code, line number, or select an option below :
Commands:  Q = Quit,  EL = Extd List,  ? = Help
```

Ventura County Library: Gateway to other services

This type of selection and navigation process is rather cumbersome compared to mouse-driven systems. It is based on the earlier days of computers when all commands had to be typed in. Nevertheless, it is that most commonly used by libraries around the world, and a little practice on the local library system is a good idea as preparation for further exploration on the Internet.

BULLETIN BOARDS

On-line bulletin boards, known also as BBSs, provide a means for kindred spirits to share information by connecting their computers over telephone lines. They were among the first popular forms of interconnection, and although their monster brethren, the on-line services, have tended to overshadow them, a large number still flourish and perform useful services.

Again the means of connecting is through the modem. At the other end of the telephone line is the bulletin board's modem, which like the library will have a welcome page that appears when the connection has been established. The following is a typical start-up after you have found a BBS number (here a fictitious one). In your communications program you call the number, having first switched on your modem and started your program:

ATDT555-3839

This dials you in. After some squeaks from your modem you see on your screen:

CONNECT 28800
Press RETURN twice to connect
You have connected to a FirstClass System. Please log in . . .

Here you enter the name you would like to use and your suggested password.

UserID: Herring
Password: Lutenist
Do you wish to register as a new user? Yes
Please answer the following questions:
Enter your first name: Albert
Enter your last name: Herring
Postal address: 2410 Farnsberry Lane, Shiptown, VT
Telephone number: 555-0319
FAX number: 555-0332
Your UserID is: Herring
Your Password is: lutenist

Press any key . . .
Logging in . . .

After you are logged in you will be presented with a page containing instructions for using the various services, a typical one being the ability to *download* free software—that is, transfer the data from the BBS to your home computer:

1 MailBox
2 Conferences
***3 News**
4 Help Folder
5 Files
6 SIGs & Chapters
7 OneNet Folder
8 LAMG Info Folder
***9 Premium Services**
***10 New User Info**
Type an item's name or number to open it.
Commands: Help, Logout, Scan.

This was the first offering from a local Macintosh user's group. The offerings are self-explanatory, but note the typical "New User Info" section, as well as the section for help. Typing the number followed by the return key brings up the item. For instance, typing 5 produces the following:

1 Big Vault o' Files Folder
***2 PowerMac Software**
***3 PowerBook & Newton**
***4 Educational Files**
***5 Spreadsheet-Database**
***6 Words & Processing**
***7 The Reading Room**
***8 Updates & Demos**
***9 Telecom Software**
***10 System Software**
***11 Utilities**
***12 Programming Aids**
***13 Sound & Music**
***14 MultiMedia/QuickTime**
***15 Etcetera**
***16 Networking Aids**
***17 Hypercard Etc.**
***18 Inits, cDevs, DA's**
***19 Gameland**

*20 Fonts & Type
*21 DTP Files
*22 Art & Graphics
*23 * New Uploads *
Type an item's name or number to open it, or EXIT to exit.

Each of these numbers would produce lists of files that you can download without any extra charge. Some files might be *freeware,* a gift from a public-spirited programmer. Others might be *shareware,* where the programmer requests a donation after a trial period. Paying this fee usually has the additional advantage of access to more documentation, future upgrades, and so on, as well as the satisfaction of returning a favor. Of course, if you hate the program you are under no obligation.

There is usually a facility also for members to *upload* items of interest, transferring items from their home computers to the bulletin board library. The BBS acts as a kind of clubhouse, where files can be kept available for members and messages can be left for others (which gave rise to the name "bulletin board" in the first place). This also makes it possible for members to chat with each other by sending their comments, which appear either publicly to all participants as a typed chat session, or more privately in the form of electronic mail (E-mail) to other members of the group. Fees if any are usually modest, representing simply the cost of operating the system on a nonprofit basis. Many such groups still exist, some specializing in particular computers, such as Macintosh user groups, others focusing on particular interests such as graphics or programming. The large store of public domain freeware programs often includes demonstration versions of major commercial software programs, including many related to music.

It should also be noted that the bigger and more sophisticated boards will often supply free a software program that makes access simpler and presents the options in a more graphically pleasing form.

INTERNET SERVICE PROVIDERS

The next level up of widening communication is to connect with an Internet service provider—basically, a BBS that offers Internet services. Such a facility represents the least complicated way to communicate with the Internet, since no special software is required by the user. Usually the offerings consist of E-mail, FTP, Gopher, Telnet, and Usenet. These services are dealt with in more detail below, but in brief they enable you to:

1. Send and receive mail throughout the Internet
2. Download files from sources all over the world

3. Go "burrowing" for files of interest through a menu system
4. Connect to libraries and so on in the same way that you did to the local library but on a worldwide basis

This type of access, known as *dial-up,* is one of the least expensive ways to use the Internet, since the cost usually consists of only a modest monthly fee with no charge for the time connected. The on-line services such as America Online or Compuserve (see below) provide the same facilities, but at a higher cost. The dial-up service takes care of the software needs—you connect to them, and they connect to the Internet. But because of the extra layer of interface between you and the Net, the speed of operations is somewhat slower than the direct connection methods discussed below, and are not suitable for the most popular Internet facility of all—the World Wide Web.

ON-LINE SERVICES

The on-line services, such as Compuserve or America Online, are in fact huge bulletin boards, or combinations of specialized bulletin boards, which do much the same thing as the original nonprofit BBSs and in addition offer news updates, libraries of information, encyclopedia access, specialized chat groups with interesting personalities on line, digests and articles from many magazines, film reviews, and forums for posting messages that may be moderated by a leading authority on the topic. For these facilities there is a monthly subscription, and when more than a basic allotment of connection time (typically five hours a month) is used, there is an additional charge based on the usage time. Most services now offer a flat monthly rate for a higher price with unlimited usage.

These services are also connected to the Internet, and like the bulletin boards and service providers can offer a send-and-receive facility for E-mail. Their sophisticated and colorful interfaces make these features easy to handle. In addition, many on-line services offer technical support from the makers of major software programs in the form of files of up-to-date information answering frequently asked questions (FAQs), free updates, and so on.

The on-line services make signing up easy because they are commercial operations and are looking for new customers. Most send out free disks that include their interface software, used to make the dial-in process simple and automatic and to present their various offerings in menu format with colorful graphics. In addition, it is common for on-line services to provide an internet *browser,* the interface that allows you to access all areas from a convenient graphic environment. Also included are programs that automate the sign-up process and offer a free ten hours or so to try things out. In addition, they have toll-free support lines to help new applicants through the installation process. All you need is a modem. Here below is a practical example of signing up with a commercial service.

COMPUSERVE

Here are the results of contacting Compuserve. I already had a sign-up program, since these are frequently given out free with magazines or as part of a modem package. It turned out that I needed an agreement number and a serial number, both of which were obtained by calling Compuserve's toll-free number. Running the program brought up a form asking for basic data such as name and address. When the agreement and serial numbers were entered, the program automatically dialed Compuserve through my modem and entered my information. In return, a message came on my screen with a user identification number and a password. At this point I was able to connect to the service through another free device, the Compuserve Information Manager or CIM. Available free from Compuserve, this program presents a graphic environment for exploring the various areas of their service.

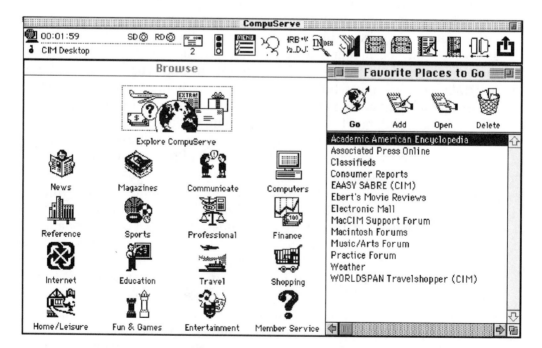

Compuserve Information Manager

To start things going, I pulled down the Services menu and searched with the word "guitar." Here is what appeared:

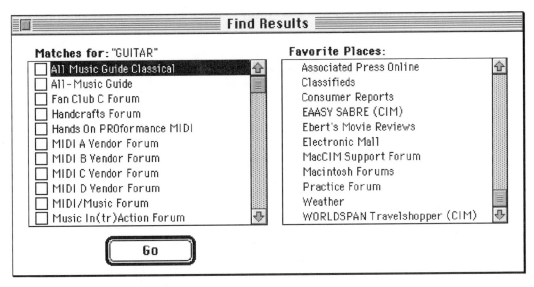

Compuserve: Browsing for guitar information

The All Music Guide Classical enabled me to track down a particular Julian Bream record by entering a series of choices related to the piece and composer. First I entered the Classical Database.

Compuserve: Database of classical records

Compuserve: Narrowing the search criteria

I clicked on **Performers** to enter my choice, and the following appeared:

Compuserve: A dialog box for choosing the desired performer

After typing in "Bream" I was offered further choices (including composer), and after negotiating these I eventually clicked on **Display Search Results** and was presented with the information below.

Compuserve: Search results

This was helpful. A search for Sor recordings produced some further results, but when I requested Weiss or Debussy nothing was found, in spite of Bream's well-known recordings of those composers.

Next I selected the Music/Arts Forum.

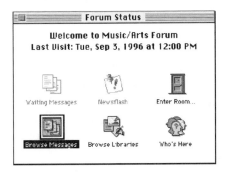

Music Arts Forum

I decided to check the library and found quite a few guitar-related items.

Filename	Title	Submitted	Size	Accesses
PBG_INFO.TXT	Product Announcement: Play Blues G...	10/27/95	3317	44
VIOLIN2.ZIP	Discussions: Violin/Fiddle Books & M...	9/30/95	11K	63
VIOLIN2.TXT	Discussions: Violin/Fiddle Books & M...	9/30/95	27.5K	51
SIGHTS.TXT	Sight-Singing	9/29/95	8729	156
MUSICIAN.TXT	Discussions: About Being a Musician	9/29/95	14.5K	135
TRUMPET.TXT	Discussion: Beg. Trumpet Tips/And O...	9/29/95	4729	114
TRIAD.TXT	Discussions: About Triads	9/29/95	9492	118
VIOLIN.TXT	Discussion: Violin Vibrato	9/29/95	8784	109
FLUTE.TXT	Discussion: Flute Embouchure/Teach...	9/29/95	16K	109
GTRBOOKS.TXT	Discussion: Guitar Method Books	9/29/95	6589	255
ASGTR.TXT	Discussion: Adult Guitar Student	9/29/95	8385	296
MOD.TXT	Modulation (or Key Change)	9/22/95	3950	167
MOCDPROG.T...	Discussion: Modulation (& More on C...	9/22/95	13K	119
EXTCHORD.ZIP	Discussion: Extended Chords (and mo...	9/10/95	24.5K	154
CHDPGUPD.T...	Discussion: Chord Progressions (Upd...	9/8/95	15.5K	301
MANDOLIN.ZIP	Discussion: The Mandolin	9/8/95	84.5K	45
HARM03.ZIP	HARMONY - a program to add chords ...	8/27/95	172.5K	128
FP2DEMO.ZIP	FretPro 2 for Windows Demo	8/27/95	93.5K	204
ABELLSON.W...	Albert Bellson, mandolin	8/26/95	6272	17
AMODEL.ZIP	A-mando wallpaper	8/24/95	47K	38
MANWAL.GIF	GIF: Mandolin Wallpaper 2	8/24/95	6102	124
F5WALL.GIF	GIF: Mandolin Wallpaper 1	8/24/95	3638	128
MANDO.GIF	GIF: Mandolin Playing Illustration	8/12/95	20.5K	67
CITY.GIF	MMG: Images and music of the city at ...	8/11/95	1M	4
BBURG4_.GIF	GIF: Brandenburg Concerto 4/1 open...	8/7/95	16K	116
CHRDPRG.TXT	Discussion: Chord Progressions I	7/29/95	5291	229

Compuserve: Music/Arts Forum Library

Naturally I was intrigued to see the file of a discussion on guitar methods. A double click with the mouse on this item enabled me to bring up the text. (The actual page is not shown here because the contributors might prefer to remain private.) The first segment was from someone planning to visit the United States from Argentina. He wanted some recommendations for guitar methods and tapes, stating that he was interested in proper notation and practice material rather than "pentagrams."

Below this block of text appeared the response—a helpful rundown of many available methods, along with a query on what he meant by "pentagrams." The conversation continued. What I was looking at was a library item (i.e., a record) rather than a live conversation, but I could have participated in a live interchange by entering the appropriate *forum*.

I moved on to select a guitar lesson. First this description appeared:

File Abstract for "GUITAR22.ZIP"

List   Info   Mark   View   Retrieve   Delete

Section: Learning/Playing   Contributer: 100574,1640   Size: 71921
Submitted: 4/16/96   File Type: Binary   Access Count: 193
Title: Ultimate Guitar Lesson v2.2
Keys: GUITAR THEORY LESSONS

The Ultimate Guitar Lesson version 2.2.

All bugs fixed.

This is a shareware guitar tuturial that applies music theory to a virtual 3-D guitar fretboad. Just click and learn.

Great for beginers Keys, hundreds of chords in many positions, modal theory and more.

Compuserve: The Ultimate Guitar Lesson

I could not look at the actual lesson without downloading it to my computer, but all I would have had to do was click on the Retrieve button. Note that the word "shareware" is used here—if you download it and find it useful, you will wish to send the modest fee to the author.

A good number of classical items of a general nature were available, as shown by the following screen. I decided to download the text file relating to sources of classical scores:

Library Files

		Filename	Title	Submitted	Size	Accesses
☐		GERGIEV.GIF	GIF: Valery Gergiev	7/27/96	62.5K	1
☐		DHVORO.GIF	GIF: Dmitri Hvorostovsky	7/27/96	95K	4
☐		HOLZMAIR.GIF	GIF: Wolfgang Holzmair	7/27/96	67.5K	4
☐		PGLASS.GIF	GIF: Philip Glass	7/27/96	65K	3
☐		JEG2.GIF	GIF: John Eliot Gardiner	7/27/96	82.5K	5
☐		BORODINA.GIF	GIF: Olga Borodina	7/27/96	78K	4
☐		STORES.TXT	Sources for Classical Scores, Sheet ...	7/15/96	5069	806
☐		KONTAKTE.TXT	Stockhausen Society Kontakte 1 1988	7/14/96	35K	12
☐		BOULEZ.GIF	GIF: Pierre Boulez	7/13/96	92.5K	8
☐		CHUNG.GIF	GIF: Conductor Myung-Whun Chung	7/13/96	95K	4
☐		GORCH.GIF	GIF: Galina Gorchakova	7/13/96	87K	9
☐		JEG.GIF	GIF: John Eliot Gardiner	7/13/96	94K	3
☐		KBATTLE.GIF	GIF: Kathleen Battle	7/13/96	86.5K	17
☐		KNUSSEN.GIF	GIF: Oliver Knussen	7/13/96	98.5K	1
☐		LEVINE.GIF	GIF: James Levine	7/13/96	72K	6
☐		MAKOLN.GIF	GIF: Musica Antiqua Koln	7/13/96	95.5K	9
☐		MUTTER.GIF	GIF: Anne-Sophie Mutter	7/13/96	91K	34
☐		ORPHEUS.GIF	GIF: Orpheus Chamber Orchestra	7/13/96	102.5K	5
☐		OTTER.GIF	GIF: Anne Sofie von Otter	7/13/96	96.5K	14
☐		PIFFARO.GIF	GIF: Piffaro - The Renaissance Band	7/13/96	80K	5
☐		PIRES.GIF	GIF: Maria Joao Pires	7/13/96	82.5K	3
☐		PLETNEV.GIF	GIF: Mikhail Pletnev	7/13/96	85.5K	1
☐		POGO.GIF	GIF: Ivo Pogorelich	7/13/96	81K	4
☐		POLLINI.GIF	GIF: Maurizio Pollini	7/13/96	128.5K	4

Browsing "Classical/Opera [2] "

Icons: Info, **Abstract**, Mark, View, Retrieve, Delete

Compuserve: Downloadable text and GIFs

I clicked on the item and was presented, as before, with a brief description of the file:

File Abstract for "STORES.TXT"

Icons: List, Info, Mark, View, Retrieve, Delete

Section: Classical/Opera [2]   Contributer: 71600,300   Size: 5069
Submitted: 7/15/96   File Type: Text   Access Count: 806
Title: Sources for Classical Scores, Sheet Music, Books
Keys: CLASSICAL MUSIC STORES SOURCES SCORES PARTS SHEET BOOKS MAIL

A list of sources for familiar and unfamiliar classical scores, parts, sheet music, and books about music, in print or out of print, in North America and Europe. Most or all do business by mail, telephone, and/or fax. Recommended by Music & Arts Forum members.

Compuserve: Downloading from a library

A click on the Retrieve button was sufficient to set the download in motion, and in a few seconds the document was in my computer. A confirming message appeared on my screen.

Compuserve: File retrieval complete

In addition to a multitude of text files, a large number, those marked *GIF*, were pictures. The on-line services provide the necessary software to display the picture files on your computer when they have been downloaded. The GIF format was in fact developed by Compuserve.

The Music Industry Forum produced the following choice of library items, with quite a few related to the guitar.

Compuserve: More guitar items

Homespun Tapes, for instance, is the label for Happy Traum's finger-picking and other instructional tapes. *Guitar* magazine has many down-loadable articles in the popular field, and information on Gibson guitars is available from the manufacturer. For the classical guitarist there is less of interest in this particular forum, but probably some items could be found.

AMERICA ONLINE

I decided to navigate my way through America Online (AOL for short) as well. This on-line service has an inviting and easy-to-use interface and an impressive array of services. Public figures, including musicians, are featured on line for chat and to answer questions from subscribers. The emphasis of course is on pop music; David Bowie is an example of the type of top-flight artists who have appeared on AOL.

The AOL software is necessary to use the service. This is widely dis-tributed free with computer magazines, or can be obtained in the United States by calling (800) 827-6364. When you have loaded the software, it guides you through the process of opening an account. Once your setting up is completed, starting your AOL program is simply a click of the mouse. After the usual modem squeaks this is what you see:

America Online: Welcome!

Choosing the main menu gets you this page:

AOL's main menu

Browsing through the options, I came across Craig Anderton's Sound, Studio, and Stage, which looks like this:

Craig Anderton's Sound, Studio, and Stage

Since Craig is the author of *MIDI for Musicians,* one of the first and best books on the topic, I expected interesting areas to explore, and indeed found many. Other interesting corners were the Composer's Coffeehouse and the Guitar SIG (Special Interest Group). Here are windows from each that help to explain their scope.

Composers' Coffeehouse

The Coffee house is a full-service area for anyone interested in making music. It's the central location on AOL to hang, whether you're into traditional composition, songwriting for the record industry, lyric writing, file & video scoring, net jamming, producing, or any aspect of the composition business. Whether you're an amateur or a pro, IBM or Mac user, we're hoping you'll find the Coffeehouse the hippest place to share tips and ideas, network, get help on the "B" section, upload your work, discuss songwriting, or just

America Online: Composer's Coffeehouse

About The Guitar SIG

The Guitar Sig

Welcome to the America Online GUITAR special interest group!

Whether you are a guitar player, student, teacher, pro, amateur, or just like listening to the instrument, this is the area for you!

This area is dedicated to all things guitar. All styles are represented here- Jazz, classical, rock, country, bluegrass, folk, blue, and many more.

The Guitar SIG (special interest group) is meant as a resource for guitarists of all styles and levels of proficiency. We hope to provide guitarists with facilities for their needs-whether it is functioning as a learning center, or a source of Tablature/Sheet music; whether a place of networking, or to just hang out and spark discussions on who your favorite guitar player is,.. this is Guitar city.

   The Guitar SIG is a "living" area, and you will undoubtedly see many changes as time goes by. We are always interested in hearing from you and listening to your suggestions on how we can make this a better place. If you don't see a representation of your style or interest here, we strongly encourage you to upload something to the libraries or tp post messages on the bulletin board that is indicative or representative of your interests. As with most areas on America Online, it is the member participation that makes them what they are!

America Online: The Guitar SIG

E-MAIL with America Online

I have found AOL's E-mail handling particularly convenient because of their "Automatic AOL" feature. After starting up their program I can activate this feature from the Mail menu.

```
┌─────────────────────────────────────┐
│ Mail  Members   Window              │
├─────────────────────────────────────┤
│ Compose Mail              ⌘M        │
│ Read Mail                 ⌘R        │
│ Address Book                        │
├─────────────────────────────────────┤
│ Read Offline Mail                   │
│ Set Up Automatic AOL...             │
│ Run Automatic AOL...                │
├─────────────────────────────────────┤
│ Dictionary                          │
│ Thesaurus                           │
├─────────────────────────────────────┤
│ Mail Center                         │
│ Mail Controls                       │
└─────────────────────────────────────┘
```

America Online: Checking for E-mail

When I choose **Run Automatic AOL,** the program does the following:

1. Automatically dials AOL through my modem.
2. Checks for my mail. If it finds new mail it announces audibly, "You have mail!"
3. Downloads the mail to my hard drive.
4. Signs off.

The whole procedure normally takes less than a minute and enables me to read the letters at my convenience without running up connect time fees. (Of course, this was more relevant in the days before AOL offered an untimed monthly rate.) In addition, I can compose replies that can be sent immediately or stored to be sent automatically at the next session. The mail check can also be set up to take place independently, as is explained in one of the help windows.

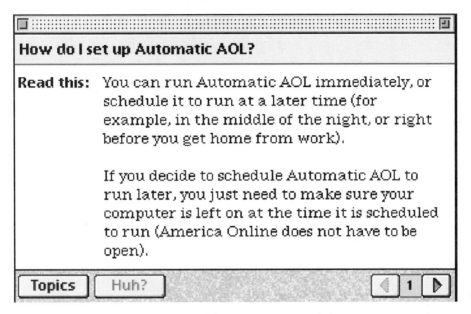

America Online: Automatic mail options

On-line services have their place, although that place is not particularly to serve the classical musician. Film reviews can be as easily found on the Internet, as can much of the software manufacturers' information and demonstration programs. The forums and chat groups associated with the various special interest groups will interest some, but the newsgroups of the Internet are far more numerous, with a place for almost every conceivable special interest. I personally use AOL for their convenient mail handling, but for most other on-line needs I prefer direct access to the Internet. Services with huge memberships can function sluggishly at peak use hours, and waiting for features to appear on the screen can become extremely tedious. But this is an area of almost daily change, and new ways to keep the membership entertained will no doubt be devised.

EIGHT
CONNECTING UP

The Internet has quite an intriguing and unlikely background. Back in the Cold War days of the 1960s, military communications were in danger of complete dislocation in the event of a nuclear strike. The reason was that the links in the network were chained in a point-to-point fashion such that a direct hit on one link could disrupt the overall connection. In these circumstances it would seem more reliable to use AT&T, but when your messages concern blowing up the world, something more private is needed.

The problem became one of those considered by the Rand Corporation, the foremost military think tank of the period. There a group led by Paul Baran came to the conclusion that a network should be connected not in a point-to-point fashion but crisscrossed in such a way that the elimination of any connection point or *node* would leave the others unaffected. In addition, the system should be digital, thus easily handled by computers, and each message should contain instructions that would enable it to find its own way to its destination. Like a postcard, it would have an address, a message, and information about the sender in case it could not be delivered.

This excellent plan was not immediately accepted by the military, but under the aegis of the Department of Defense an experimental network, the ARPANET, was formed, linking four university campuses for the primary purpose of allowing scientists to share information. Paul Baran's self-routing messages, known now as *packets,* became the E-mail of today and one of the most popular and widely used features of the ARPANET.

The story from then on is of continual growth. The network spread first to more campuses, still mainly for the use of scientist and academics, becoming international in 1973 with connections to England and Norway. In 1979 the first Usenet newsgroups were formed to discuss a huge range of topics beyond academic confines. The TCP/IP, a universal language for Internet computers, was developed by a team led by Bob Kahn and Vint Cerf. This made it possible for users to be freed from the awkward Unix commands originally necessary for networking.

In 1991 a team at the University of Minnesota led by the computer programmer Mark McCahill released Gopher, the first point-and-click way of navigating the files of the Internet. Originally designed for campus communications, Gopher software was distributed without charge and became very popular on the Internet. McCahill called it "the first Internet application my mom can use."

As usage became easier the Net widened still further, spreading from primarily campus use to the general public through subscription connection services. The year 1991 saw a major step forward in ease of use with the development of the graphic browser and the hypertext language that is at the heart of it. The browser is dealt with extensively below, since it is now the most widely used form of accessing the Internet.

Thus a military need spawned an academic network that grew hugely to attract a vast popular membership throughout the world. The growth is so fast that it is impossible to quote numbers with any hope of accuracy, but the number of users is many, many millions and still growing fast.

The Internet is one of the most compelling attractions of investing in a personal computer. All the on-line services combined contain only a minuscule fraction of what is available on the Net, and the Net has no "per hour" charges. A huge amount of material exists out there, described by some as an information highway and by others as a sea of garbage. Both descriptions have some truth, and the art of using the Internet consists of separating the two. Mere *surfing,* as random wandering is described, can result in a tremendous waste of time. But as the Net grows, so do the search systems and lists of resources, and the use of these aids can help enormously in finding areas of true interest.

The first step is to make the necessary physical connection. The required tool to connect with any network is the modem. The process is the same as that described above for reaching bulletin boards or the local library, but in this case the connection is to a *service provider,* which is connected to the Internet and can handle the necessary operations to enable you to use the standard services. The simplest form of link, as mentioned in the previous chapter in connection with bulletin boards, is known as a *dial-up* connection. As with the basic bulletin board, you follow screen instructions and menu choices to access the features that interest you.

STANDARD SERVICES

E-mail

Electronic communication is possible with anyone who uses the Internet and has an address. It is probably the most popular usage of all, since there are no extra charges for sending and receiving mail. E-mail through on-line services such as America Online is described in the previous chapter, but in fact any service provider can give you an address and the means to send and receive mail. E-mail, which travels at lightning speed whether across town or around the world, is very reliable and free of charge.

In addition to the text of the letter, separate files may be attached. This compares to sending files with a communications program as described in the previous chapter, but is easier to use for most people since there is no need to choose the protocol, such as Zmodem, that is to be used. In most cases the attachment of a file is a simple matter of a few mouse clicks.

FTP

File Transfer Protocol is a way to access and download to your computer files that are stored by Internet member sites. There are huge numbers of sites from which text files and programs can be downloaded, including demonstration programs from software manufacturers. Technical information and upgrades are also widely available, and most of this is free. Specialized programs exist, such as the very popular Fetch, for using the FTP facility; however, Internet browsers can also be used, making it very simple for those who use the World Wide Web.

Gopher

Gopher is a facility for searching through interlinked menus for files of interest existing on the Internet. Before the establishment of the World Wide Web, this was one of the favorite search tools. Gopher sites link to other sites throughout the world, and it is possible to roam through *Gopherspace* in a fashion similar to roaming the World Wide Web.

Telnet

Telnet is a way to connect into the computers of other organizations, such as libraries. When connected via Telnet, the distant computer responds to your typed-in commands and takes control of your screen to explain commands and options. This way of exploring the holdings of distant libraries is similar to the process described in chapter 7 for reaching your local library, but the Internet makes it possible to extend this facility all over the world.

Newsgroups

Newsgroups are special interest groups where members can post requests for information and messages of interest to other members. The messages and requests often stimulate comments and further discussion.

Access to these newsgroups, known generically as the Usenet, is afforded by your service provider, which also performs a convenient function in storing for you a list of the newsgroups that you find interesting. You can "subscribe" to any of the thousands of groups that have interest for you. This does not mean that you have to pay a subscription—like so much on the Internet, the Usenet charges no fees—but simply that your chosen groups will be kept as a short list for easy access. When you use this facility you have the opportunity through your software to choose groups for your subscription list, either by picking from the huge total list or by knowing from some source the name of the group that you want.

The World Wide Web

All of the above facilities can now be combined into one convenient interface that includes the capability of exploring the *World Wide Web*. The Web is a fascinating series of screens, or *pages,* that are joined together with graphics and sound by an interlinking system known as HTML (Hypertext Markup Language). Under this system certain words are underlined as key words, and clicking on one of these brings up a new screen. The new screen may be from the same source or may be a link to somewhere totally different, perhaps the other side of the world. The interface that presents all this material is known as a *Web browser.* Browsers are now appearing that offer convenient access to newsgroups, E-mail, FTP, and Gopher in addition to the ability to roam the World Wide Web.

To use the World Wide Web, a translation program needs to reside in your computer to convert the commands you send into a form understandable by Internet computers. The older access systems involved keyed-in commands based on the Unix language; these were inconvenient to use and memorize for the occasional user. Now the translation program vastly simplifies the whole process. The catch is that this involves a specialized link to your service provider, for which there is usually a higher fee than for basic service. This special link enables you to be connected directly into the Internet, which is essential to enjoying the full capabilities of the Web. The technical term for this link is an *SLP/PPP connection,* and this will be good enough for most general users. However, there is an even faster *ISDN connection,* which involves the installation of a special line by the local telephone company. The problem is that any calls on this line will be charged by the hour, and this cost, together with the expense of installation, makes such a system impractical for most noncommercial users.

INSTALLING INTERNET SOFTWARE

Service providers will make the connection process as easy for you as possible. Most will supply the software that needs to reside on your computer and will provide technical support by telephone until you are successfully on line. The programs are different for PC or Macintosh computers, but essentially all you have to do when everything is properly installed is to command the software program to dial your service provider. From that point everything is automatic, your modem dials out, and at the end of the connection process you see a message on your screen that you are on line.

Once connected, you may choose individual programs to handle E-mail, newsgroups, and so on, or you may choose an all-in-one browser such as Internet Explorer or Netscape. For most uses you will probably choose the browser, since this is the easiest approach and will give you access to the World Wide Web, the area of the Internet that is developing most rapidly. Many of the illustrations that follow use the Netscape browser, since that is the one that I personally use, but this is not to say that others do not exist that work very well, and new ones will probably have appeared by the time you read this. Also, the programs dedicated to E-mail or newsgroups (such as Eudora or Newswatch, respectively) tend to offer more facilities than the all-in-one browser, so in time you may wish to have these as an alternative. Most Internet software can be downloaded free or as shareware, so this does not represent additional cost. To make a start, however, it is easier to use the one simple interface and to experiment with the various facilities.

NEWSGROUPS WITH A WEB BROWSER

Newsgroups are part of the *Usenet,* a vast area of interlinked bulletin boards of specialized interests. Most people think of it as part of the Internet, since Internet service providers are usually also news servers, but in fact it is a network of its own. The newsgroups compare to the special interest groups of the on-line services but are far more numerous and varied.

The easiest way to grasp any of the functions we have discussed is to travel through a practical session with actual examples of the screens that appear. Our first such "journey" will be to a newsgroup, since for many guitarists this will be the major interest area.

At this point I have found and subscribed to a service for a SLP/PPP connection, or I have subscribed to America Online, Compuserve, or an equivalent on-line service. I have installed the necessary software (provided to me as part of the service) to make the link work, and now I am ready to make the connection. I have already put the necessary phone numbers into the software (or my provider did before sending it over), so now all I have to do is make sure that my modem is properly connected and switched on and give the command to dial out. If all goes well I will be hearing the dial sounds, followed by an assortment of squawks and rushing sounds as information is exchanged with the modem at the other end. This will be followed by an indication on my screen that the connection has been established.

Although many excellent programs specialize in newsgroups, I am using the Netscape browser because of its ability to handle the many aspects of networking, and because of its widespread, free availability.

For the first excursion I will start up Netscape.

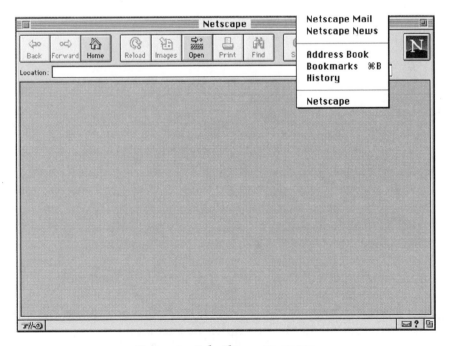

Netscape: Selecting newsgroups

After I choose **Netscape News** from the menu, the page below appears. I have made the menu choice **Show All Newsgroups,** and these have appeared on the left of the screen, sorted into category groups that can be opened by clicking on the triangular symbols at the left margin. When clicked, the symbol turns sideways and the sublist is revealed. Since there are thousands of groups, this type of sorting really helps.

Netscape: Showing all newsgroups

You will now want to choose the groups that particularly interest you for your "subscribed" list. This way you can keep track of when new messages appear and whether you have already read them.

For the classical guitarist the obvious place to start is the newsgroup **rec.music.classical.guitar,** and I have been through the process of selecting this group for my subscribed list. All that was involved was to click against the relevant groups in the check mark column. When I next start up, these groups will appear instead of the vast total list.

Here is my new startup list:

News Server	✔	Unread	...
▽ 🖳 news.fishnet.net (default news host)			
🗐 rec.music.classical.guitar	✔	10	32
🗐 rec.music.classical	✔	146	1...
🗐 rec.music.compose	✔	59	59
🗐 rec.music.early	✔	24	24
🗐 rec.music.classical.recordings	✔	89	89

Netscape: Subscribed newsgroup list

A click on the appropriate group, and this is what appears:

News Server	✔	Unread	...
▽ 🖳 news.fishnet.net (default news host)			
🗐 rec.music.classical.guitar	✔	10	32
🗐 rec.music.classical	✔	146	1...
🗐 rec.music.compose	✔	59	59
🗐 rec.music.early	✔	24	24
🗐 rec.music.classical.recordings	✔	89	89

Subject
▷ 🗐 "Piano" tone. Any recommendations.
▷ 🗐 — Reading Music —
🗐 **Re: 10-string guitar – HUH?!**
🗐 **Re: Afro-Cuban Lullaby by Brouwer?**
🗐 Better Classical Guitar Designs ?
▷ 🗐 **Re: Damage to guitar while changing strings?**
🗐 Good CG Shops in Central London?
▷ 🗐 Re: Looking for a music notation software
🗐 **Musical Stylings**
▷ 🗐 **Rest Stroke**
▷ 🗐 Segovia-Ponce letters
🗐 Re: Some Thoughts on Sight Reading
🗐 Re: Total Guitar Issues 1 - 20
🗐 Vicente Tatay Spanish Flamenco guitars

Netscape: A page from rec.music.classical.guitar

Each of the topics with a triangle beside it is a *thread*, that is, a continuing series of postings as different people express their comments.

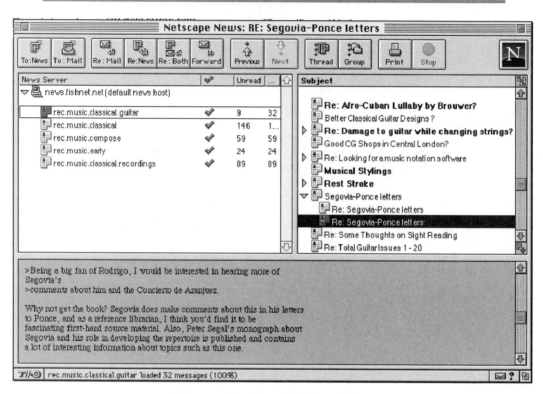

Netscape: The Segovia/Ponce letters

The newsgroup screen has three parts: one for viewing the groups, one for the list of messages, and finally one spelling out the selected message. These are all adjustable with the mouse and behave somewhat like roller blinds. When first exploring this interface it is a good idea to practice the various resizings, as these are necessary for comfortable reading of the appropriate segment. In the above example all segments are shown as a demonstration of the complete process, but to read the messages it is more convenient to push up the horizontal center divider to give more space to the message.

TYPES OF MESSAGE

In a specialized group like this the level of interest of the postings is usually quite high. There is a wide variety of levels of expertise, from beginners seeking advice to helpful guidance from experienced professionals. For instance, as I go through I notice the name of a famous musicologist, one of whose monumental works is in my library, so I check his contribution and find that he is answering a request for sources of recordings of music by Luis de Narvaez. Requests for information are often posted, and the answers are often very enlightening.

SENDING YOUR MESSAGE

When you encounter a posting that interests you, you can either direct your response via E-mail to the individual who made the posting or, if your information is likely to be of general interest, post it publicly for the whole group. With Netscape making a reply is very simple. You choose **Mail** from the Message menu, and a convenient letter form appears on your screen, already addressed to the person who made the posting.

```
┌─────────────────────────────────────────────────────────────┐
│ ▫️▪️  ≡≡≡  Re: Lord Herbert of Cherbury's Lute Book ≡≡≡    ◰ │
├─────────────────────────────────────────────────────────────┤
│ ┌────────┬───────┬────────┬─────────┐ ┌──────┐                │
│ │SendNow │ Quote │ Attach │ Address │ │ Stop │                │
│ └────────┴───────┴────────┴─────────┘ └──────┘                │
│ Subject: │Re: Lord Herbert of Cherbury's Lute Book         │  │
│ ▽ Addressing                              Attachments         │
│ ┌──────────────────────────────────────┐┌──────────────────┐ │
│    Mail To: anon@wherenet.net                                 │
│       Cc:                                                     │
│                                                               │
│                                                               │
│                                                               │
│ Dear lutenetters!                                             │
│ >  >                                                          │
│ > >I am looking for a source of Lord Herbert of Cherbury's    │
│   Lute Book, preferably                                       │
│ > >as a facsimile edition. Can anybody help me?               │
│ > >Thank You                                                  │
│ >                                                             │
│ Lord Herbert of Cherbury's Lute Book MU.MS. 689 is not        │
│ available in a facsimile edition. You can write the           │
│ Fitzwilliam Museum and purchase a microfilm or photographs:   │
│                                                               │
│ Fitzwilliam Museum                                            │
│ Trumpington St.                                               │
│ Cambridge, UK CB2 1RB                                         │
│                                                               │
└─────────────────────────────────────────────────────────────┘
```

Replying to a request for information

As a convenience, the previous message (the one you are answering) is automatically put in the > quotes favored by the Usenet. The reply will be posted at the bottom of the particular thread of messages that have appeared on this topic.

If I had wished to reply personally I would have chosen the **Mail Reply** option from the Message menu. To reply on the newsgroup (i.e., for all to read) I would choose **Post Reply.** Note that all that it takes to post the message is a click on the Send Now button.

MAILING LISTS

Mailing lists serve a purpose similar to that of the newsgroups, the difference being that the messages, instead of being posted to a public board, are mailed to your personal E-mail address. The advantage of this system is that junk messages are filtered out by the moderator, and the focus is thus on the primary interest of the group. The only disadvantage is that if you belong to several groups your mailbox can become overfilled, and you need to decide with every letter whether to read or delete it, since otherwise it will remain there, with the numbers building up. As a solution, many mailing lists, including the one illustrated below, offer the postings in digest form, that is, a periodic mailing of the accumulated messages for a period in one file.

The Classical Guitar Mailing List

One group that I belong to is concerned with lute music and performance. The address is **lute@cs.dartmouth.edu,** and a person wishing to

join would send an E-mail message to **lute-request@cs.dartmouth.edu.**
Topics include forthcoming concerts, discussions on technique, lutes for
sale or wanted, new record information, and so on.

The mechanism for reading the letters in Netscape is similar to that
for viewing newsgroup postings. However, when I have read a letter I can
permanently delete it, so that the incoming mail file does not become too
large or disorganized. Alternatively, I can drag its icon from the list on the
right to the Save icon on the left, where it can be accessed at any time.

Dragging a letter to the Save file

Both newsgroups and mailing lists represent a good way to keep in
touch with colleagues on a worldwide basis. For instance, today's mail
included postings from Lithuania, Germany, and Costa Rica directed to
this U.S.-based list. Always two addresses appear, that of the list server
and the private E-mail address of the contributor. As with newsgroups
you have the choice of replying privately or writing to the list server
address for delivery to all members.

A SESSION WITH FTP

The File Transfer Protocol is a simple way of transferring files from one
computer to another. Most often it is used to download information or
programs from Internet sites. The distant site will have an address beginning with the letters *ftp* such as this one: **ftp://ftp.arcetri.it/pub/fron-
imo.** This is in fact the location for Francesco Tribioli's lute tablature
program entitled Fronimo. There have been many complimentary reports
about this program on the newsgroups, saying that it is easy to use, prints
excellent-looking tablature, transposes from Italian tablature to French
and vice versa, and even plays the tablature as MIDI. The FTP address
was also given for a downloadable demonstration version. All that needs
to be done is to enter the address into Netscape.

```
┌────────────────────────────────────────────────────────────────────────┐
│ ▪▪▪                          Netscape                               ▪▪ │
├────────────────────────────────────────────────────────────────────────┤
│  ⇦o      o⇨      🏠        ©        🖼       ⇨o      🖨      🔍      ●      │ N │
│  Back  Forward  Home     Reload    Images   Open    Print   Find    Stop   │
├────────────────────────────────────────────────────────────────────────┤
│ Location: [                                                            ] │
├────────────────────────────────────────────────────────────────────────┤
│                                                                          │
└────────────────────────────────────────────────────────────────────────┘
```

Netscape address line

After I press the return key to start things going, here is what appears:

```
┌────────────────────────────────────────────────────────────────────────┐
│ ▪▪▪          Netscape: Directory of /pub/fronimo                    ▪▪ │
├────────────────────────────────────────────────────────────────────────┤
│  Back  Forward  Home   Reload  Images  Open  Print  Find   Stop    │ N │
├────────────────────────────────────────────────────────────────────────┤
│ Location: [ftp://ftp.arcetri.astro.it/pub/fronimo/                     ]│
├────────────────────────────────────────────────────────────────────────┤
│ Current directory is /pub/fronimo                                        │
│ ─────────────────────────────────────────────────────────────────────── │
│ Mon Dec 16 21:20:32 1996                                                 │
│                                                                          │
│ Welcome, ftp@port057.vta.fishnet.net! This is an experimental FTP server.│
│ If have any unusual problems, please report them via e-mail              │
│ to root@sisifo.  If you do have problems, please try using a             │
│ dash (-) as the first character of your password -- this will turn       │
│ off the continuation messages that may be confusing your ftp client.     │
│                                                                          │
│ 1 of 10 maximum allowed users are currently logged on.                   │
│ ─────────────────────────────────────────────────────────────────────── │
│ Up to higher level directory                                             │
│    borron1.mid        3 Kb    Wed Dec 20 00:00:00 1995 audio/x-midi      │
│    fronimo.zip      395 Kb    Tue Apr 23 00:00:00 1996 application/x-compressed│
│    pkunzip.exe       28 Kb    Mon Sep 18 00:00:00 1995 Binary Executable │
│                                                                          │
└────────────────────────────────────────────────────────────────────────┘
```

FTP: Arriving at the Fronimo site in Italy

All that remains is to click on the words "fronimo.zip" and the download process starts. This is a PC file, and the "zip" suffix indicates that a popular method of compressing the file has been used to lessen the time of the transfer. In case you do not have the necessary program to "unzip" Fronimo, this is made available also simply by downloading "pkunzip.exe." Overall the process is simple and automatic.

Uploading your file to a distant site is better done with a dedicated

FTP program such as Fetch. Although the uploading process is quite straightforward, the general user rarely needs to do it, and thus it is not discussed in detail here.

TELNET

Using Telnet to visit distant libraries is practically the same process as the simple dial-up visit to the local library described in chapter 7. Fortunately, it is not necessary to dial long distance, since the connection can be made through your local server or on-line service. To operate Telnet you need a simple program to handle the session. Commonly available examples are NCSA Telnet for the Macintosh and Ewan for the PC. The session below uses the NCSA program.

A PRACTICAL TELNET SESSION

After making the connection to my service provider and starting NCSA Telnet, I choose the File menu as a first step. Alternatively, I could have typed the Telnet address into my Netscape browser, which would then have opened NCSA Telnet.

The **Open Connection** command brings up a dialog box, and I type in the Telnet address. On this occasion I have chosen to visit the Oxford University libraries.

Entering a Telnet address

Almost immediately, although on this occasion at a distance of about six thousand miles, the following screen appeared:

```
╔══════════════════ library.ox.ac.uk 1 ═══════════════════╗
║                                          OLIS Message System
║                      Welcome to OLIS
║
║ Welcome to the new OLIS.  This is the OLIS message system.  News and important
║ messages are displayed here.  When you have finished reading the messages you
║ may proceed into OLIS.
║
║ When you have finished, leave the OPAC by typing 'OFF' at the OPAC menu screen.
║
║    ─────────────────────────────────────────────────────
║
║    Use 'c' to continue into the catalogue. Use + and - to go up and down
║    pages. Use the arrow keys and enter to select one of the following
║    items.
║
║      1. Terminals dedicated to OLIS (Advance) OPAC
║
║    ─────────────────────────────────────────────────────
║
║ Commands: Use arrow keys to move, '?' for help, 'c' to continue into OLIS.
╚══════════════════════════════════════════════════════════╝
```

Telnet: Welcome to Oxford

From here on it was simply a question of following the instructions on the screen. After each choice is made, the Enter key is pressed for the operation to take place. In this case I typed a *c* and was presented with a choice of libraries within the OLIS system. I chose the library of the Music Faculty.

```
╔══════════════════ library.ox.ac.uk 3 ═══════════════════╗
║         OLIS - The Oxford Libraries Information System
║
║   7 Bodleian Japanese Library      24 History of Art
║   8 Bodleian Law Library           25 Hooke Science Lending Library
║   9 Brasenose College              26 Indian Institute
║  10 Chinese Studies Library        27 Inst. of Economics & Statistics
║  11 Clarendon Laboratory           28 Jesus College
║  12 Classics Lending Library       29 Keble College
║  13 Computing Laboratory           30 Lady Margaret Hall
║  14 Continuing Education Department 31 Latin American Centre
║  15 Corpus Christi College         32 Lincoln College
║  16 Criminological Research Centre  33 Magdalen College
║  17 Earth Sciences                 34 Maison Francaise
║  18 Eastern Art Library            35 Materials Department
║  19 Educational Studies            36 Mathematical Institute
║  20 Engineering Science            37 Middle East Centre
║  21 English Faculty                38 Modern Languages Faculty
║  22 Experimental Psychology        39 Museum of the History of Science
║  23 History Faculty                40 Music Faculty
║
║      Type your choice or Q or <Return> to see more:
╚══════════════════════════════════════════════════════════╝
```

Selecting a library

The available commands are clearly stated, and at the time I made the connection the whole process worked smoothly and surprisingly fast considering the amount of miles and the number of computers involved. For instance, typing the *f* for forward was almost as fast as normal typing, although the appearance of the letter was in fact an echo from the distant computer.

```
╔═══════════════ library.ox.ac.uk 1 ═══════════════╗
║        WELCOME TO OLIS: the Oxford Libraries Information System        ║
║                                                                        ║
║  Use arrow keys to highlight selection, then enter search terms        ║
║  Or type command, then enter search terms e.g. t=moby dick             ║
║                                                                        ║
║  Look for the First Word(s) in:        Look for Keyword(s) in:         ║
║                                                                        ║
║  Title            t=                   Title Keyword        tw=        ║
║  Author           a=                   Author Keyword       aw=        ║
║  Subject          s=                   Subject Keyword      sw=        ║
║  Journal Title    jt=                  Notes                nw=        ║
║  All Indexes      all=                 All Keywords         w=         ║
║                                                                        ║
║                                        Number Searches:                ║
║                                        ISBN/ISSN            i=         ║
║  Highlight for:                                                        ║
║  Further search options (second screen)                                ║
║  Borrower information, e.g. books on loan, fines, etc.                 ║
║                                                                        ║
║  Press Return for more help or type E and press Return if you wish to Exit ║
║  Lute music█                                                           ║
║                                                                        ║
║  Enter the main subject term                                           ║
╚════════════════════════════════════════════════════════════════════════╝
```

The search options

After making my choice of lute music, I was presented with chances to narrow the search.

```
╔═══════════════ library.ox.ac.uk 1 ═══════════════╗
║              Online Catalogue - Heading Browse                         ║
║  Retrieved Subjects: S=Lute music - manuscripts                        ║
║                                                                        ║
║     Subject Heading                               Number of Titles     ║
║   1. Lute music -- History and criticism     (LCSH)        6           ║
║   2. Lute music -- Hungary -- 16th century -- History (LCSH)   1       ║
║      and criticism                                                     ║
║   3. Lute music (Lutes (2))                   (LCSH)        1           ║
║   4.   [See Also Narrower Term] Suites (Lutes (2)) (LCSH)   0           ║
║  >>>                                                                   ║
║   5. Lute music -- Manuscripts                (LCSH)        2           ║
║   6. Lute music -- Manuscripts -- Catalogs    (LCSH)        1           ║
║   7. Lute music -- Manuscripts -- Thematic catalogs (LCSH)  1          ║
║   8. Lute music -- Periodicals -- Indexes     (LCSH)        1          ║
║   9. Lute music -- Thematic catalogs          (LCSH)        1          ║
║  10. Lute music -- To 1800                    (LCSH)        2          ║
║  11. Lute -- Performance                      (LCSH)        1          ║
║                                                                        ║
║  ...Continued...                                                       ║
║  Options:    Enter lines (e.g. 1 or 1,2 or 1,2,4 or 1-4 or 1,3-4 etc.) ║
║  # line(s)   Forward   Backward   Previous screen   Search jump        ║
║  Modify search   Review search   OPAC parms   New search   Quit search ║
║  Output #(s)                                                           ║
╚════════════════════════════════════════════════════════════════════════╝
```

Narrowing the search

From here I chose number 5, for manuscripts, and after making my selections eventually came upon what was the original object of my search, David Lyons's bibliography *Lute, Vihuela, and Guitar to 1800*.

```
╔══════════════════════════════════════════════════════════════╗
║ ▓▓        library.ox.ac.uk 3                                ▓▓ ║
║      ░░Online Catalogue - BRIEF DISPLAY░░    (1 of 1 titles) ▲ ║
║                                           Number of holdings :1 ║
║  AUTHOR        :Lyons, David B.                                ║
║  TITLE         :Lute, vihuela, guitar to 1800, a bibliography / ║
║  SUBJECT       :Stringed instruments -- Bibliography          ║
║                 Lute music -- Bibliography                    ║
║                 Vihuela music -- Bibliography                 ║
║                 Guitar music -- Bibliography                  ║
║  SERIES        :Detroit studies in music bibliography ; 40    ║
║  PUBLISHER     :Information Coordinators,                     ║
║  DATE          :1978                                          ║
║                                                               ║
║      LIBRARY    LOCATION    SHELFMARK            STATUS       ║
║      -------    --------    ---------            ------       ║
║   1. MusicF     MUS Main Libr Bibliography/REF.ONLY          ║
║                               ML128.G8.LYO                    ║
║                                                               ║
║                                                               ║
║  Last Page                                                    ║
║  Options: █ Display item/piece record █                      ║
║   ▓#item▓  Full display  Previous screen  Extend search  Limit list ║
║   Output   Reservations  Review search   OPAC parms   New search ║
║   Quit search                                                 ║
╚══════════════════════════════════════════════════════════════╝
```

Locating the Lyons bibliography

I also found an interesting thesis by Julia Craig-McFeely on English lute manuscripts and scribes, 1530–1630. Further investigation revealed that both text and pictures from this thesis can be accessed at **http://www.cs.dartmouth.edu/~wbc/julia**. See below for how to do this.

```
╔══════════════════════════════════════════════════════════════╗
║ ▓▓        library.ox.ac.uk 1                                ▓▓ ║
║      ░░Online Catalogue - BRIEF DISPLAY░░    (1 of 1 titles) ▲ ║
║                                           Number of holdings :6 ║
║  AUTHOR        :Craig-McFeely, Julia                         ║
║  ADDED AUTHORS :University of Oxford. Faculty of Music. Thesis ║
║  TITLE         :English lute manuscripts and scribes, 1530-1630 / ║
║  SUBJECT       :Lute music -- England -- 16th century -- Manuscripts ║
║                 Lute music -- England -- 17th century -- Manuscripts ║
║                 Lute music -- Manuscripts                     ║
║  DATE          :1994                                          ║
║                                                               ║
║      LIBRARY    LOCATION    SHELFMARK            STATUS       ║
║      -------    --------    ---------            ------       ║
║   1. Bodley     BOD Bookstack MS. D.Phil. c.11047 (v. Available ║
║                                1)                             ║
║   2. Bodley     BOD Bookstack MS. D.Phil. c.11048 (v. Available ║
║                                2)                             ║
║   3. Bodley     BOD Bookstack MS. D.Phil. c.11049 (v. Available ║
║                                3)                             ║
║   4. MusicF     MUS Main Libr English music (Vol. 3)         ║
║   ...Continued...                                             ║
║  Options: █ Move forward █                                   ║
║   #item  ▓Forward▓  Full display  Previous screen  Extend search ║
║   Limit list  Output  Reservations  Review search  OPAC parms ║
║   New search  Quit search                                    ║
╚══════════════════════════════════════════════════════════════╝
```

Locating a thesis on early English lute manuscripts

I was also able to learn about library hours, copy availability, and so on—information that would have been invaluable advance preparation for a trip to Oxford in which time might be limited.

Although the system worked comparatively smoothly, the total process was time-consuming, owing to the necessity of parading back and forth between the various screens. This sort of operation is much faster when mouse or hypertext driven. Later we will compare this visit to a similar one on the World Wide Web and get an impression of the speed and efficiency of the different paths.

THE WORLD WIDE WEB

We now come to the part of the Internet that is currently far and away the most popular and widely visited. I say visited rather than used, since a large part of the Web would come under the heading of decorative rather than functional. The individual screens are referred to as *pages,* and those that represent the initial introduction of an individual or organization are known as *home pages.* On the home pages are underlined items, known as *links;* a click of the mouse on one of these takes the explorer to either another page of the original host or to a completely different location, perhaps on the other side of the world. All of this is happening through your modem via your service provider, which connects you to the Internet.

Whereas the services mentioned above can be accessed through simple specialized software, such as the popular Eudora for E-mail, to use the Web you need a browser. Fortunately, these can be obtained either free or for minimal cost. Many service providers supply browsers as part of the start-up package. The one used here is again Netscape, which includes the facility for handling newsgroups, as explored above.

A PRACTICAL WORLD WIDE WEB SESSION

The first step is to go on line by making the connection to your service provider. Starting up the browser will produce a default page, perhaps blank or that of your provider. Let's start with a blank.

Starting up Netscape

At this point the all-important item is the line following the word "Location," since this is where the address of the desired destination must be typed in. Most Web addresses begin with the prefix *http://* which identifies the type of message (hypertext transfer protocol) to the Internet, and many are followed with the letters *www* to indicate a World Wide Web address. As a simple start I will type the address of the Guitar Foundation of America, since the foundation's Web site contains links to a number of pages of guitar interest. The addresses are called URLs (pronounced *earls*), standing for Uniform Resource Locators.

Here is what appears when I type in the URL for the foundation and press the Enter key:

The Guitar Foundation of America home page

The delightful logo figure appears in bright reds and oranges. Each of the underlined items on the left represents a link to another page, and all that is necessary to reach and open that page is to click the mouse on the underlined item. If the link sends you to another location, the URL for that location will appear in your address line. Here, for instance, is a linked page showing other guitar societies that have their own pages. A click on any of these transfers you instantly to the new location.

Guitar Societies Online

- Fort Worth Classical Guitar Society New! Christopher McGuire, Artistic Director
- Baltimore Classical Guitar Society New! Mike Kirkpatrick, 4607 Maple Ave. Baltimore MD 21227
- Classical Guitar in Colorado Colorado Specific Classical Guitar Links, by Jeff Kenyon
- Calgary Classical Guitar Society 60 Berkley Close, N.W., Calgary, Alberta ,Canada T3K 1B3
- Columbus Guitar Society Karl Wohlwend, 3372 Broadmoor Ave, Columbus, OH 43213
- Connecticut Classical Guitar Society New! Penny Phillips, P.O. Box 1528 Hartford CT 06144
- Edmonton Classical Guitar Society #111 - 5125 Riverbend Road Edmonton, Alberta Canada, T6H 5K5
- Northwest Classical Guitar Society David Feingold, 1809 Summit St Belllingham WA 98225
- Philadelphia Classical Guitar Society Joe Mays, 2038 Sansom St Philadelphia PA 19103
- Portland Guitar Society Jeff Elliot, P.O. Box 15253 Portland OR 97215
- South Texas Classical Guitar Society Larry Bailey, P.O. Box 2111 McAllen TX 78502
- Tidewater Classical Guitar Society Sam Dorsey, P.O. Box 1171 Norfolk VA 23501
- Hong Kong Guitar Information Alliance
- Japanese Classical Guitar Society
- Sydney Classical Guitar Society
- Victoria Guitar Society

The Guitar Foundation of America: Links to other societies

Let's explore some of these links. As a first stop let's try the individual artist pages:

Solo Artists

Badi Assad	Ernesto Bitetti
Julian Bream	Bream Discography
Giovanni DeChiaro [New!]	Jan-Olof Eriksson
Ricardo Iznaola	Dale Kavanaugh
Gerald Klickstein	Norbert Kraft
John McClellan	Anders Miolin
Christopher Parkening	David Russell
Maria Sanchez-Cortes	Michael Cedric Smith
David Starobin	David Tanenbaum
Scott Tennant	John Williams
Bill Yelverton	

Ensembles

Guitars A Quattro [New!]
Ricardo Filipo & Duda Anízio [New!]
Amadeus Guitar Duo
Amsterdam Guitar Trio
Los Angeles Guitar Quartet
The Newman & Oltman Guitar Duo

Guitar Foundation, Individual artist pages

A click on Julian Bream produces the following:

CLASSICS WORLD
BIOGRAPHY

Julian Bream

guitar

Acclaimed as the greatest guitar and lute virtuoso of the 20th century, Julian Bream was born in London in 1933. He received musical training at the Royal College of Music in London, and made his public performance debut at the age of seventeen. His technique and sensitivity to diverse musical styles quickly made him a popular favorite of audiences all over the world, and he enjoyed critical raves for his performances of medieval music and contemporary compositions.

In 1960, Mr. Bream founded the Julian Bream Consort, an ensemble of original instrument virtuosi that has experienced unprecedented success in their chosen oeuvre. Under his direction, the group has done much to revitalize interest in the music of the Elizabethan era.

Julian Bream was named an Officer of the Order of the British Empire in 1964, and a Commander of the Order of the British Empire in 1985.

Julian Bream (© 1996 by BMG Music)

Turning to the ensemble group, a click on Los Angeles Guitar Quartet produces the following:

The Los Angeles Guitar Quartet

Notice that in neither case do the pages have anything to do with the Guitar Foundation; they are simply included on the foundation's page as the means to reach these other points of interest.

Another click takes us to Katunori Shiota's Classical Guitar Page in Japan, which has much interesting material, including information on the Guitar Cultural Hall. The host of this page is shown with his wife, and below an extract from the very comprehensive presentation about the hall.

Katunori Shiota and his wife

The Guitar Cultural Hall

In this hall, <u>you can see the history of these precious guitars.</u> Guitars from the early vihuela to those of Mr Torres's period, have been restored by Mr Marcerino Lopes, and are displayed in chronological order. In an <u>exquisite instrument room</u>, we display guitars made by craftsmen from the 18th century to the present day.

A crafted guitar is made of the best woods chosen from all over the world, and seasoned naturally for ten years. Although a violin consists of 70 parts, a guitar consists of 360 parts, so guitar makers can only make one-fifth as many instruments as violin makers; it is said that a guitar maker makes about 300 guitars in their lifetime. In a <u>workshop exhibition room</u>, you can handle the guitar parts and learn how to make them. There is a <u>Japanese-style seminar room</u> for training or at which participants can stay overnight. We are <u>proud of the acoustics of the Hall</u>, and are sure that its wooden structure will appeal to you. You can use it not only

Japan's Guitar Cultural Hall

A jump to Hong Kong via **http://www.hk.super.net/ ~ hkgia/** results in the pleasant sounds of Bach while you read the page of the Hong Kong Guitar Information Alliance (GIA). It includes a collection of photographs from a class with John Williams.

A class with John Williams in Hong Kong

Another page of interest to guitarists is that of the Villa-Lobos museum in Brazil. Information includes biography, pictures of the composer, forthcoming festival, and so on. The English-language page has recently been added.

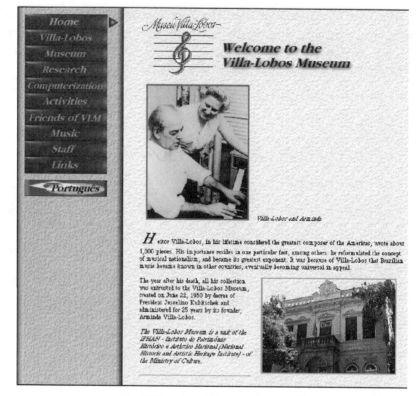

The Villa-Lobos Museum in Brazil

Irresistible also to the guitar enthusiast are Brian Bergstrand's fan pages for Andrés Segovia and Fernando Sor:

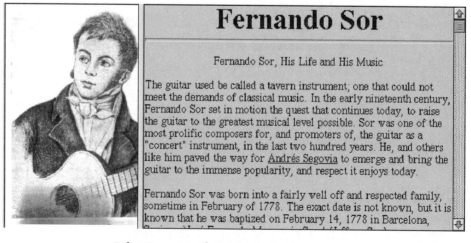

Brian Bergstrand: Fernando Sor home page

144

At the same time I couldn't resist a glance at his Andrés Segovia page:

Brian Bergstrand: Andrés Segovia home page

For lute enthusiasts a first stop is at the Lute Society of America's home page. The extensive catalog of microfilms available to members can be downloaded from here.

The Lute Society of America home page

A click on "The Lute Page" link brings up a splendid collection of pictures of historic paintings with lutes. Modern lute information is also available, as well as information about Wayne Cripps's lute tablature program.

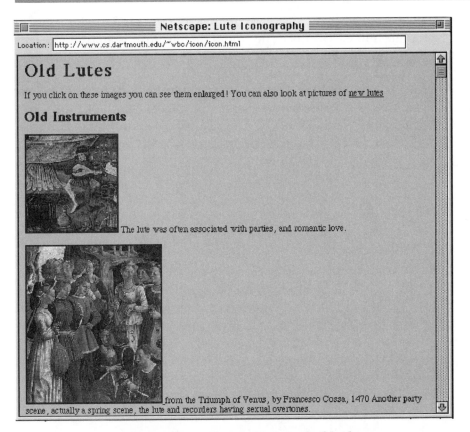

The Lute Page: Many gorgeous graphics here

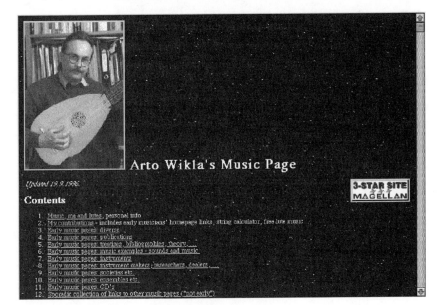

Arto Wikla home page

One of the older sites on the Net is that of Arto Wikla, who runs an interesting lute and early music site from Finland. Arto is an example of a dedicated amateur who gives much time and enthusiasm to updating and improving his pages.

By now you can see how easy it is to travel from point to point on the World Wide Web. In just this one session I traveled through links provided by the Guitar Foundation of America to points in Finland, Brazil, Japan, and Hong Kong. On the Web, distance is really no object, and the truly worldwide character becomes quickly apparent.

NINE
BUILDING YOUR HOME PAGE

One of the more practical uses of the Internet for the professional player is to spread the word about services he or she may be offering.

The example given here is for a fictitious George Fretworthy, a guitar teacher in Nearville, who plays professionally at weddings and other festive occasions in addition to periodic concert appearances. For him the Internet is an excellent way to advertise in a creative and personal way at a modest cost. Many service providers offer the ability to put up a personal page as part of the monthly fee paid for basic service. While the advertisement can reach only those who use the Net, that population is increasing by leaps and bounds, and for those not connected it is easy to go to a friend's house to check for special items or services.

LEARNING HTML

If we suppose that George is connected through a typical server offering the free page, his first step is to become familiar with the language that will make his page appear with text and graphics. This language is the Hypertext Markup Language (HTML), a simple set of coded commands that govern the appearance of the page and enable links to other pages. George could pay someone to do this for him, but doing so could be quite expensive and make him dependent on someone else whenever he wanted to make changes. If he can read music, he is unlikely to have problems with the HTML language. Books exist for fast learning, such as Laura Lemay's *Teach Yourself Web Publishing with HTML in a Week*. In addition, the Netscape and other browsers have a menu item that will reveal, and save if necessary, the HTML code for anyone else's page, making it simple to copy and personalize an appealing presentation.

A PRACTICAL EXAMPLE

Let's suppose that George wants to show a picture of himself to announce his availability for concerts, weddings, and so on, and also to promote his private teaching. What he has in mind looks approximately like this:

George's home page

In HTML that page looks like this:

HTML source page

```
< html >
< title > George Fretworthy Guitar Home Page < /title >
< body >
< center > < h1 > George Fretworthy < /h1 > < /center >
```

```
< center > < img src = "George.gif" > < /center > < p >
```
This page contains information about George Fretworthy's guitar
    recitals, his teaching schedule, and availability and rates for
    weddings etc.
```
< h4 > < a href = "Biog.htm" > About George Fretworthy
    < /a > < /h4 > < p >
< h4 > < a href = "Recital.htm" > Current Recital
    Program < /a > < /h4 > < p >
< h4 > < a href = "Weddinfo.htm" > Booking music for your wed-
    ding! < /a > < /h4 > < p >
< h4 > < a href = "Teaching.htm" > My Teaching
    Schedule < /a > < /h4 > < p >
```
Telephone (805) 555-6742
```
< b > Email < /b > @ alo.com" > < b > gfretfman@ alo.com < /b >
< /body >
< /html >
```

The following brief explanation shows how comparatively simple the language is:

<html> identifies this as a hypertext markup language page. The page must start this way to be recognized as HTML.

<title>. Almost all simple instructions are inserted inside the angle brackets. When the instruction ends, it is canceled by a slash with the same instruction, in this case **</title>.** This identifies the text in between as being the main title of the page. In most browsers this appears above the actual page in a special title area. Note that the **<html>** instruction is also switched off at the bottom of the page with **</html>.**

** <h1> George Fretworthy</h1> **

<center> centers what follows until switched off with **</center>.**

<h1> sets the text to the largest headline size. Higher numbers indicate smaller text. This presents George's name prominently at the top of the page

<img src="George.gif">. This instruction causes the picture saved with the file name *George.gif* to appear on the screen, centered because of the prior instruction.

<p>. This makes a paragraph separation to make space before the next item.

<a href="Biog.htm">About George Fretworthy </a>. The **<a** instruction is an important part of the language, since it instructs the browser to jump to another page, in this case a file saved as *Biog.htm.* Following this are the words that will appear highlighted on the original screen. A click of the mouse on this highlighted text brings up the new page with George's biography on it. This new file will behave in exactly the same way as the original page and will contain links to George's other information pages and back to his home page. The other pages would be prepared in exactly the same way as the home page, with title, body, and so on.

This is in fact all that is necessary for the preparation of a simple home page. The only "extra" item is the picture of George, which needs to be scanned and saved in a format (*.gif* or *.jpeg*) recognizable by the browser. For those who don't own their own scanners, it would be necessary to find a friend who has one or a commercial service. In larger towns the latter are usually listed as service bureaus in the Yellow Pages, and the scan can be made for a modest price. As the rest of the page costs nothing at all to make, the overall cost is still a bargain.

The final step is for George to deliver a disk to his service provider with the necessary set of files. The home page will probably be called *Index1.htm* by convention. The *.htm* suffix denotes a text HTML page. The other files will be named exactly as they appear on the home page, such as *Biog.htm* and *Recital.htm*. The service provider will take over from there and give George a form of address (URL) for his home page. This will be something like **http://www.netserver.com/ ~ fretworthy/.** The first part simply defines what follows as hypertext on the World Wide Web; then comes the server's name, followed by George's identification. When typed into the browser, this address will bring up George's *Index1.htm* home page.

The example given above will actually work, and substituting names and pictures would result in a functioning page.

TEN

GOING SHOPPING ON THE NET

M uch of interest to the musician may be found in an Internet shopping excursion. At the time of writing, the trip is likely to be one of window shopping rather than completed buying, owing to the public's unease about feeding credit card numbers into such a widely accessible medium. In addition to providing better privacy and security, the Net has yet to plant this perception into the public's mind. In many cases, however, all that is necessary to complete a purchase is to make a separate telephone call to a toll-free number. This sort of buying is useful when shopping for a book, sheet music, strings, and so on. Obviously, it does not apply to expensive items such as guitars, which must be seen and tested. Nevertheless, background information can be found to begin a guitar search.

GUITARS

In researching guitars it is a good plan to have a specific target in mind so as not to waste too much time. For a very fine instrument it will be worth looking for individual makers and those who deal in handmade instruments. For makers a start could be made at the Guitar Foundation of America page. Here is their current list, with a link to the larger collections at "Richard's List of North American Luthiers" and "Luthiers Around the World."

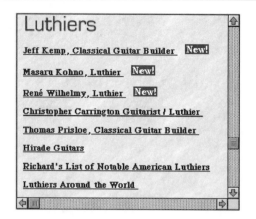

Luthiers

Jeff Kemp, Classical Guitar Builder **New!**

Masaru Kohno, Luthier **New!**

René Wilhelmy, Luthier **New!**

Christopher Carrington Guitarist / Luthier

Thomas Prisloe, Classical Guitar Builder

Hirade Guitars

Richard's List of Notable American Luthiers

Luthiers Around the World

Guitar Foundation of America: Luthier listing

Famous Guitarmaker Internet World Headquarters

Luthiers Around the World

An alphabetical listing of luthiers listed by geographical location. If you would like us to include your name on this list, contact Gitarmkr@CyboZone.com .

Australia	Canada	England	Germany	Holland
Iceland	Ireland	Italy	North Ireland	South Africa
Spain	Sweden	Switzerland	. . .	

Luthiers . . . Get on the WEB NOW!

United States of America:

Alabama	Hawaii	Massachusettes	New Mexico	South Dakota
Alaska	Idaho	Michigan	New York	Tennessee
Arizona	Illinois	Minnesota	North Carolina	Texas
Arkansas	Indiana	Mississippi	North Dakota	Utah
California	Iowa	Missouri	Ohio	Vermont
Colorado	Kansas	Montana	Oklahoma	Virginia
Connecticut	Kentucky	Nebraska	Oregon	Washington
Delaware	Louisiana	Nevada	Pennsylvania	West Virginia
Florida	Maine	New Hampshire	Rhode Island	Wisconsin
Georgia	Maryland	New Jersey	South Carolina	Wyoming

Luthiers listed at :http://www.cybozone.com/fg/luthier.htm

The lists grow all the time, and by the time you read this Luthiers Around the World will probably include even more countries. The listings here are not links but a means of contacting the instrument makers by mail or telephone.

```
┌─────────────────────────────────────────────────────────────┐
│ ▣      Netscape: Richard's List of Luthiers           ▣       │
├─────────────────────────────────────────────────────────────┤
│ Location: http://www.maui.net/~rtadaki/luthierlist.html       │
├─────────────────────────────────────────────────────────────┤
│ Tom Blackshear                                            ⬆   │
│ 17303 Springhill                                              │
│ San Antonio, Texas 78232                                      │
│                                                               │
│ R. E. Bruné                                                   │
│ 800 Greenwood Street                                          │
│ Evanston, Illinois 60201                                      │
│                                                               │
│ Gregory Byers                                                 │
│ 15000 Hearst Rd.                                              │
│ Willits, California 95490                                     │
│                                                               │
│ Douglas Ching                                                 │
│ 11405 Misty Arbor Pl.                                         │
│ Chester, Virginia 23831                                       │
│                                                               │
│ David Daily                                                   │
│ 1425 Greenbrae Drive                                          │
│ Sparks, Nevada 89431                                          │
│                                                               │
│ Lester DeVoe                                                  │
│ Long Look Farm                                                │
│ 568 Paris Hill Rd.                                        ▣   │
│ South Paris, Maine 04281                                      │
│                                                               │
│ Jeffrey Elliott                                               │
│ 2812 S. E. 37th Ave.                                          │
│ Portland, Oregon 97202                                        │
│                                                               │
│ Thomas Humphrey                                               │
│ 124 West 72nd Street, 2C                                      │
│ New York, NY 10023                                            │
│                                                               │
│ Paul Jacobson                                                 │
│ 21112 E. Clover Hills Rd.                                     │
│ Cleveland, Missouri 64734                                     │
│                                                               │
│ Jose Oribe                                                    │
│ 2141 Lakeview Rd.                                             │
│ Vista, California 92084                                       │
│                                                               │
│ Richard Prenkert                                              │
│ P. O. Box 3266                                                │
│ Santa Rosa, California 95402                              ⬇   │
├─────────────────────────────────────────────────────────────┤
│ ▣                                                    ✉ ?  ▣   │
└─────────────────────────────────────────────────────────────┘
```

Richard's List of Luthiers (partial)

Richard's List of Luthiers is focused on North American makers and includes links to those who have Web sites. Here, for instance, is the result of clicking on the link for José Oribe:

José Oribe home page

José Oribe: An elegant rosette

Lute makers also well represented on the Internet. A page from Arthur Robb has pictures, prices, and even lute jokes.

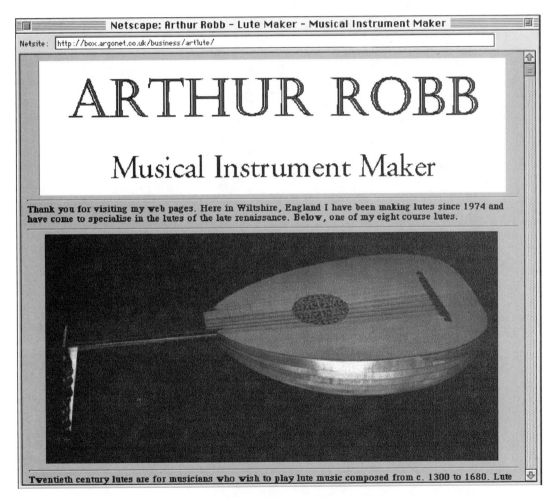

Arthur Robb home page

Crossing the line between custom makers and manufacturers is the comprehensive list from Web Guitar Resources, an extensive and popular site maintained by Chris Bray since June 1995.

Web Guitar Resources: Manufacturers and Luthiers

From here it is an easy jump to learn more about Takamine Guitars.

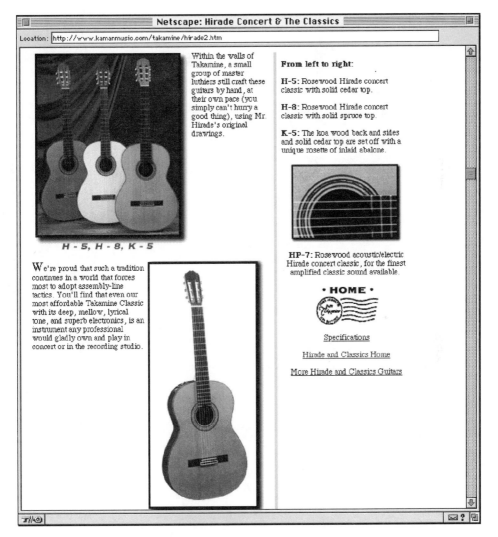

Netscape: Hirade Concert & The Classics

Location: http://www.kamanmusic.com/takamine/hirade2.htm

Within the walls of Takamine, a small group of master luthiers still craft these guitars by hand, at their own pace (you simply can't hurry a good thing), using Mr. Hirade's original drawings.

H - 5, H - 8, K - 5

We're proud that such a tradition continues in a world that forces most to adopt assembly-line tactics. You'll find that even our most affordable Takamine Classic with its deep, mellow, lyrical tone, and superb electronics, is an instrument any professional would gladly own and play in concert or in the recording studio.

From left to right:

H-5: Rosewood Hirade concert classic with solid cedar top.

H-8: Rosewood Hirade concert classic with solid spruce top.

K-5: The koa wood back and sides and solid cedar top are set off with a unique rosette of inlaid abalone.

HP-7: Rosewood acoustic/electric Hirade concert classic, for the finest amplified classic sound available.

• **HOME** •

Specifications

Hirade and Classics Home

More Hirade and Classics Guitars

Hirade Guitars from Takamine

GUITAR DEALERS

Dealing in guitars at the highest level, we can jump from the Guitar Foundation page to the Guitar Salon in California. This site has guitars from the world's finest makers.

Netscape: Classical Guitars---GSI: Classical and Flamenco Guitars

Location: http://www.guitarsalon.com/inventory/newclassical.html

GSI

Guitar Salon International

3100 Donald Douglas Loop North
Santa Monica, California 90405 U.S.A
Phone : 310 - 399 - 2181 Fax : 310 - 396 - 9283

Classical Guitars

image available   image not available

1996 Kevin Aram---Due 10/96
Spruce top, Indian back and sides
Scale length: 650mm (England)
(Hauser Model)

One of the most sought after luthiers in Europe, Aram makes this instrument in the style of Hauser. It is very finely crafted, using excellent European spruce, Rodgers tuners, and French Polish method for the finish. This is a very traditional instrument with a bold, clear and -- at the same time-- earthy sound. It is very easy to play and has a nice, smooth response. Due 9/96

1987 René Baarslag---$4,500
Spruce top, Indian back and sides
Scale length: 650mm (Spain)

An excellent Granada-style instrument with very good volume, tone and workmanship. This is an easy guitar to play with a Torres type of sound. Finish is French Polish and the soundboard is well aged. I consider this an excellent value for a delightful, first rate concert instrument which would also serve beautifully for recording.

1966 Marcelo Barbero (Hijo)/Arcangel Fernandez---$6,800
Spruce top, Indian back and sides
Scale length: 650mm (Spain)

Actually, the label reads: "Marcelo Barbero (Hijo) por casa de Arcangel Fernandez." In 1966, Marcelo Barbero (Hijo) was in his early 20's. This instrument was made by Marcelino and Arcangel together. It has a wonderfully dark sound, with very bold basses and strong trebles. It sounds very much like an old spruce top Miguel Rodriguez (at less than half the price). This guitar is also very fast, like a good flamenco and very fun to play.

Guitar Salon International

160

A similar top-level operation in New York can also be visited from the Guitar Foundation link:

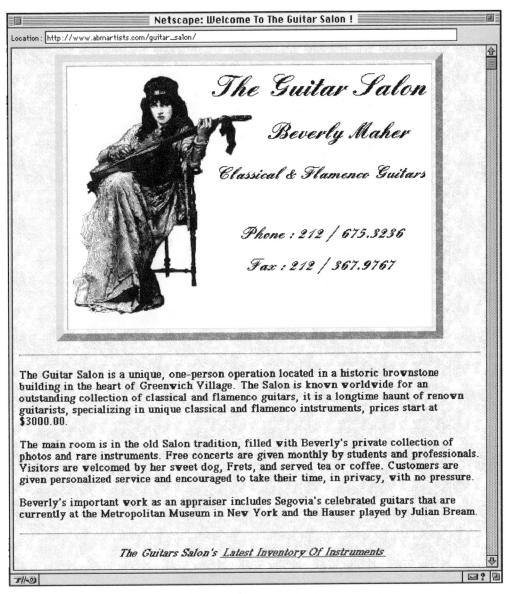

Beverly Maher's Guitar Salon

At the time of writing this site had a mouth-watering list of guitars in inventory from the world's greatest makers.

THE VIRTUAL GUITARIST

In a different field, an interesting site for unusual and hard-to-find instruments is presented by "Lark in the Morning" of Mendocino, California.

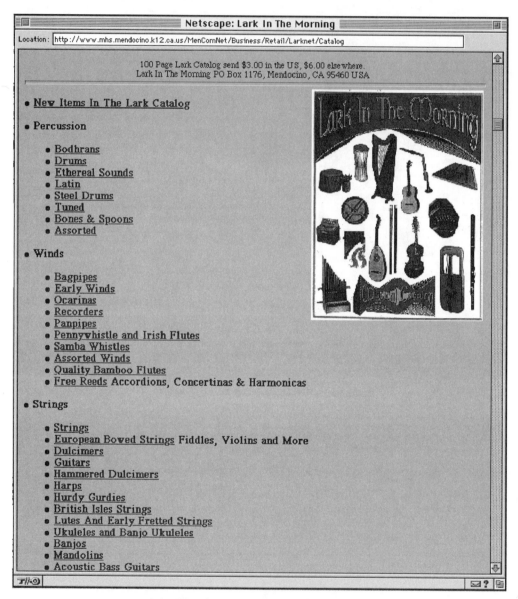

Lark in the Morning: Unusual offerings galore

SHEET MUSIC AND BOOKS

Books are probably one of the easiest items to find on the Internet, particularly in the United States. Going to the largest first, one might well visit Amazon.com, which claims to be the "largest bookstore on Earth"!

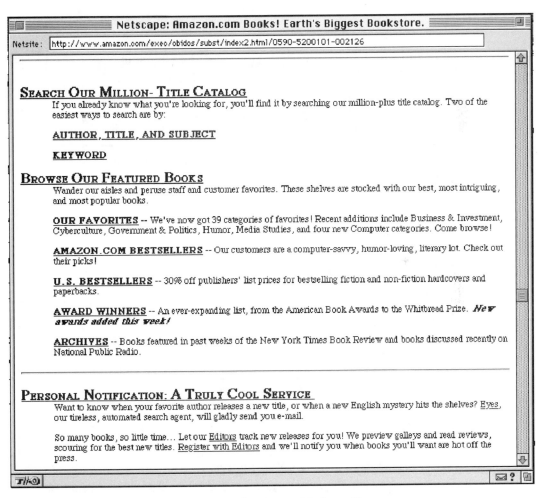

Amazon Books: General Information

Many of the large music publishers have a Web presence. One of the best organized in the United Kingdom is Music Sales Ltd., which enables you to search their complete catalog, as shown below. For sheet music a fax service is available (within the United Kingdom only) where buyers first look up the catalog numbers, then follow instructions on the telephone for immediate faxback of the music.

Music Sales Ltd.: The Shop Window

In the United States, the Guitar Gallery of Houston has an extensive guitar music catalog, which may be explored on the spot or downloaded as a file. This company is also a source of guitar strings and accessories.

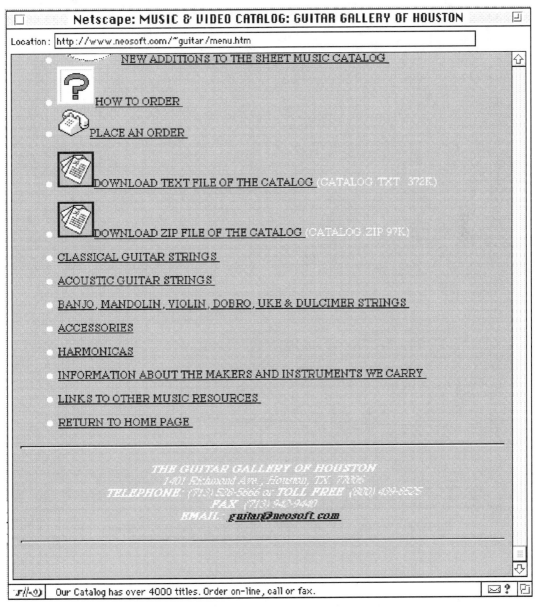

The Guitar Gallery of Houston: An impressive site

```
╠▓╣  Netscape: MUSIC & VIDEO CATALOG CONTENTS: GL ╠▓╣
```

```
⇦o        o⇨        ⌂         ⟳          ▨        ⇥°        🖨
Back    Forward    Home     Reload    Images    Open     Print          N

Location: http://www.neosoft.com/~guitar/contents.htm
```

```
(13)  BASS GUITAR-MUSIC                                            ⬆
(14)  BEGINNING GUITAR-MUSIC
(15)  BLUEGRASS GUITAR-MUSIC
(16)  BLUES GUITAR-MUSIC
(17)  CLASSICAL GUITAR
  (a)  CLASSICAL GUITARMETHODS & STUDIES-MUSIC
  (b)  CLASSICAL GUITARCOLLECTIONS-MUSIC
  (c)  CLASSICAL GUITARSOLOS-MUSIC
  (d)  CLASSICAL GUITARDUOS-MUSIC
  (e)  CLASSICAL GUITARTRIOS-MUSIC
  (f)  CLASSICAL GUITARQUARTETS-MUSIC
  (g)  CLASSICAL GUITARQUINTETS-MUSIC
  (h)  CLASSICAL GUITARSEXTETS-MUSIC
  (i)  CLASSICAL GUITAR& FLUTE-MUSIC
  (j)  CLASSICAL GUITAR& RECORDER-MUSIC
  (k)  CLASSICAL GUITAR& VOICE-MUSIC
  (l)  CLASSICAL GUITAR& VIOLIN-MUSIC
  (m)  CLASSICAL GUITAR& MANDOLIN-MUSIC
  (n)  CLASSICAL GUITAR& CELLO-MUSIC
  (o)  CLASSICAL GUITAR& OTHER INST'S-MUSIC
  (p)  CLASSICAL GUITAR& PIANO-MUSIC
  (q)  CLASSICAL GUITARCONCERTOS-MUSIC
  (r)  CLASSICAL GUITAR"LITURGICAL"-MUSIC
  (s)  CLASSICAL GUITARARRANGEMENTS OF POP TUNES-MUSIC
  (t)  CLASSICAL GUITARFLAMENCO-MUSIC
(18)  CHRISTMAS GUITAR-MUSIC
(19)  FINGERSTYLE GUITAR-MUSIC
(20)  JAZZ GUITAR-MUSIC
(21)  ROCK GUITAR-MUSIC
(22)  SONGBOOKS
(23)  MISC                                                         ⬇
```

The Guitar Gallery of Houston: Detail of the guitar music categories

On my own site you may find details and contents of my instruction books and anthologies. Also, a demonstration version of SpeedScore is available for download:

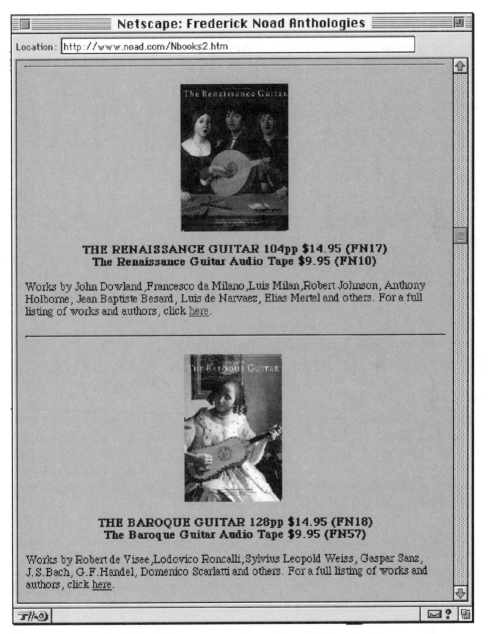

The author's home page: Part of the anthology series

A click on the underlined link brings up the table of contents. For easy purchase there is a link to D & H Sales. D & H also specialize in the works of Howard Heitmeyer:

QUOTES FROM THE GUITAR PLAYER ARTICLE

"UNKNOWN GREATS!"

Amazing Players You've Never Heard Of

"Howard Heitmeyers name should be on the role of the best guitarists, but it isn't. (In the studio) he had an amazing ability to read and interpret classical guitar, and he could memorize everything. He really impressed me with being one of the best guitarists I ever heard."

-Laurindo Almeida

"Howard Heitmeyer is one of the most dedicated musicians I've ever known. As far as we were concerned he was busy being a devout student of the guitar."

-Tommy Tedesco

"Howard took up the guitar from scratch. I've never seen anybody ever learn anything so fast in my life. He then went on to study orchestration and composition and write beautiful stuff. He could read like crazy - a total musician. He saw me struggling with a classical (guitar); he took it up and -overnight again-became outrageous. He is truly an amazing person."

-Howard Roberts

Technique Tips Video

Changing Strings, Tuning and Tidbits Video

Latin Stylings, Book and Two Videos

My Favorite Hymns Vol. 1, Music, Tablature, Audio Tape

D&H Sales: About Howard Heitmeyer

CD-ROMS

It is hard to find stores with a really extensive range of CD-ROMs. One satisfactory on-line outlet with some twenty-eight hundred titles in stock is the CD-ROM Shop in Toronto, which will ship to "anywhere on the planet." They are to be found at **http://www.cdromshop.com/cdshop/**. Here is part of their award-winning site, which contains search facilities and shopping aids:

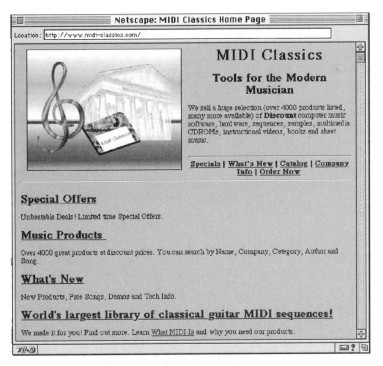

The CD-ROM Shop

MIDI FILES

For classical guitar MIDI files on disk for both Macintosh and IBM, the place to visit is Phil Sabatine's MIDI Classics.

MIDI Classics, Classical Guitar MIDI files

These few examples are enough to show the breadth of the resources available. By the time you read this the pages will be fuller, and the number of commercial offerings will have grown. If nothing else, shopping on the Internet will give you an idea of prices and availability and help you be a better-informed buyer when the time to make your purchase finally arrives.

ELEVEN

ON-LINE
SEARCHES

WEB SEARCH ENGINES

In the earlier days of the Internet, specialized search tools such as Archie, Veronica, and WAIS were the main means of finding information and files of interest. (More about these can be found at the University of Texas site at **http://www.utexas.edu/search/type.htm**.)

Search devices at the University of Texas

Now *search engines,* as they are called, have increased in efficiency and scope and tend more and more to replace the earlier devices. In fact, we have now reached a point where there are search engines for search engines, that is, pages that group many such devices so that if one does not succeed, others may be tried. A good starting point is a page by that name.

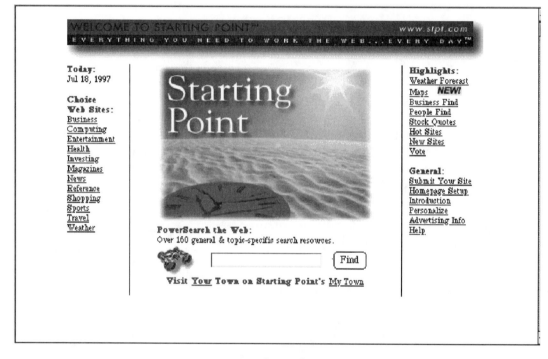

Starting Point

As well as targeting Web pages, the engines now search the newsgroups, going through thousands of documents to find a target word or phrase. To give a personal example, I sometimes find it hard to cover all the postings to the newsgroups that interest me. However, I can track a topic I am particularly following by entering a key word in Deja News (**http://www.dejanews.com**), even though it is a month later. Also, if personal questions have been directed to me I simply enter my name, and up comes a set of links to every posting that includes it. At least this way I can catch up eventually when time permits.

```
═══════ Netscape: Deja News - Power Search Form ═══════
Location : http://www.dejanews.com/forms/dnq.html
```

DEJANEWS   Home   Power Search   Post   Ask DN Wizard   Help

POWER SEARCH

Search for: `"John Dowland"`   (Find) (Clear)

⚡ **CREATE A QUERY FILTER** (to refine your search)

⚡ **SEARCH OPTIONS**

Keywords matched:	◉ All	○ Any	
Usenet database:	◉ Current	○ Old	
	10/24/96 to Now	1/1/96* to 10/24/96	
Number of hits (per page):	◉ 25	○ 50	○ 100
Hitlist detail:	◉ Concise	○ Detailed	
Hitlist format:	◉ Listed	○ Threaded	
Sort by (per page):	◉ Score	○ Newsgroup	○ Date
	○ Author	○ Subject	
Article date bias:	◉ Prefer new	○ Prefer old	
Article date weight:	◉ Some	○ Great	○ None

```
http://www.dejanews.com/dnabout.html
```

Deja News: Power Search page

Choosing as a topic the name John Dowland produced a surprising number of references, which I am sure would have amazed and gratified the Elizabethan composer.

The Lycos search engine also found a large number references on the World Wide Web. Here are just the first few:

3) Dowland: Consort Music
  Dowland: Consort Music [Cover graphic] Compact Disc CDA66010 Music by John Dowland THE EXTEMPORE STRING ENSEMBLE GEORGE WEIGAND director Contents: Sir Henry Guilford his Almain [4'33] violin...
  http://www.hyperion-records.com/..details/66010.html (2k)
  [99%, 1 of 2 terms relevant]

4) Dowland lute
  Dowland lute Dowland lute music Lute Music of John Dowland Ronn McFarlane Dorian 90148 Contents: Sir John Smith's Almain Captain Digorie Piper's Galliard My Lord Willoughby's Welcome...
  http://www.best.com/~music/musicvault/tag/catalog/cd90148.html (1k)
  [98%, 1 of 2 terms relevant]

5) Dowland songs
  Dowland songs Dowland A Pilgrim's Solace Dowland: A Pilgrimes Solace (1612), etc. The Consort of Musicke - Anthony Rooley L'Oiseau Lyre 436 188 Contents (2CDs): A Pilgrimes Solace...
  http://www.best.com/~music/musicvault/tag/catalog/cd436188.html (4k)
  [96%, 1 of 2 terms relevant]

6) Dowland songs
  Dowland songs Dowland Third Book of Songs Dowland: The Third Booke of Songs (1603) The Consort of Musicke - Anthony Rooley L'Oiseau Lyre 430 284 Contents: Fairwell, too fair (tenor...
  http://www.best.com/~music/musicvault/tag/catalog/cd430284.html (4k)
  [98%, 1 of 2 terms relevant]

7) Dowland: Lachrimae, or Seaven Teares
  Dowland: Lachrimae, or Seaven Teares [Cover graphic] Compact Disc CDA66637 JOHN DOWLAND (1563-1626) Lachrimae, or Seaven Teares THE PARLEY OF INSTRUMENTS RENAISSANCE VIOLIN CONSORT PETER...
  http://www.hyperion-records.co.uk/details/66637.html (3k)
  [96%, 1 of 2 terms relevant]

8) The Dowland HTTP Server!
  Date: Monday, 12-Aug-96 10:14:34 GMT Last-Modified: Tuesday, 16-Jul-96 17:04:26 GMT Content-type: text/html Content-length: 1723 The
  http://dowland.dcrt.nih.gov/ (2k)
  [93%, 1 of 2 terms relevant]

9) Robert Dowland: A Musicall Banquet 1610
  Robert Dowland: A Musicall Banquet 1610
  http://www.best.com/~music/musicvault/tag/performers/rnphil/caward/cdo-555.html (1k)
  [93%, 1 of 2 terms relevant]

10) The King of Denmark's Galiard John Dowland(1562-1626)
  The King of Denmark's Galiard, John Dowland The King of Denmark's
  http://hike1.hike.te.chiba-u.ac.jp/higaki/award5/ (1k)
  [93%, 1 of 2 terms relevant]

Lycos search result

Not only the title of a Web page is searched but the content as well. For instance, following up one of the links produced a review of a CD that contained a Dowland piece, although Dowland was nowhere in the heading or title.

```
┌─────────────────────────────────────────────────────────────────────┐
│ ▤▤     ═══════════  Netscape: Cherburyslutebook.html ═══════════  ▣▣ │
├─────────────────────────────────────────────────────────────────────┤
│ Location: │http://www.princeton.edu/~stmoore/Cherburyslutebook.html │ │
├─────────────────────────────────────────────────────────────────────┤
```

LORD HERBERT OF CHERBURY'S LUTE BOOK. Paul O'Dette, lute. HARMONIA
MUNDI FRANCE 907068 [DDD?]; 76:38. Produced by Christel Thielmann.

ANON: En me revenant. Chacogne. GAULTIER: Courante. Courante "Son adieu". Courante
sur "J'avois brisé mes fers". DESPOND: Filou. BACHELER: Prelude. Fantasie. Galliard upon
a galliard by John Dowland. Pavin. 3 Courantes. La jeune fillette. R. JOHNSON: Pavin.
Almaine. Fantasie. LORENZINI DI ROMA: Fantasia. CATO: Fantasia sopra la canzon degli
uccelli. C. HELY: 3 Fantasias. Sarabrand. POLONAIS: Courante sur le Courante de
Perrichon. Sarabande. HERBERT OF CHERBURY: Pavan.

Edward, Lord Herbert of Cherbury (1582-1648), ambassador to France for James I between
1619-1624, brother to the famous poet George Herbert, was a well-rounded man of many
talents, among these music. He left an extensive manuscript collection of pieces for ten-course
lute (numbering 242), including much music which he must have collected in France, and also
documenting the swan song of the lute in England. The main courses are still tuned after the
Renaissance fashion - shortly thereafter the newer French tunings would become the standard.

Paul O'Dette has made an admirable selection of music heretofore virtually unexplored on disc,
evenly divided between the French and English styles. To my ear the French works are more
pleasing than astonishing, though the anonymous Chacogne and the strummed Sarabande by
Polonais (the earliest extant sarabande for lute, according to O'Dette) make a strong impression.
The real discovery here is the music of Cuthbert Hely, who seems to have been Herbert's lute
teacher, and whose works (a total of six) survive only in Herbert's manuscript.

Diana Poulton says in *Grove* "His music is of astonishing intensity", and she's right - this is
dark and brooding music, exploring the depths of the instrument, with some remarkable
harmonies. Particularly striking is the last fantasy included here which drives its single theme
through four minutes of development. The music of Daniel Bacheler (primarily represented on
disc by his "Mounsier's Almaine") and Robert Johnson (who shared a Junghänel release with
Thomas Robinson - Accent 8121, not yet out on CD) also deserves the extended look it
receives here. O'Dette closes the disc with a composition of Herbert himself. Lord Herbert
must have been a pretty fair lutenist, to judge from his book, but his pavan rambles.

A worthy and absorbing release from one of the ornaments of our time.

-Tom Moore

```
├─────────────────────────────────────────────────────────────────────┤
│ 🖅/┃                                                          ✉ ?  🖿 │
└─────────────────────────────────────────────────────────────────────┘
```

Cherbury Lute Book, CD review

One of my favorite search engines is AltaVista, which lists the number of "hits." Here is the result of the same query:

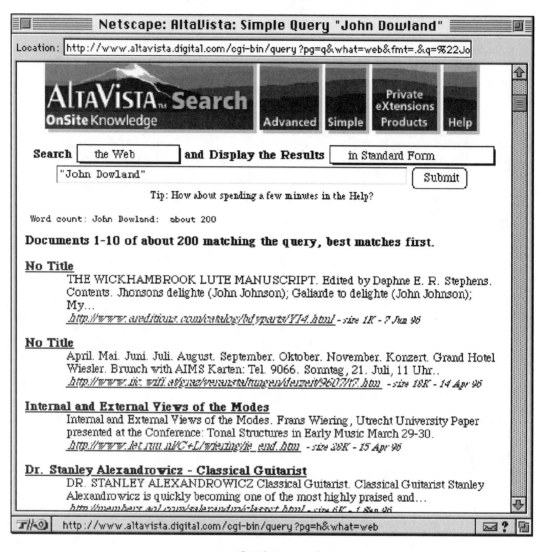

An AltaVista search.

Reproduced with the permission of Digital Equipment Corporation. AltaVista and the AltaVista logo
and the Digital logo are trademarks of Digital Equipment Corporation.

One of the most important aspects of searching is being able to narrow the search down to what you are actually looking for, since otherwise a great deal of time is wasted going through irrelevant listings. If I am trying to find out about Paul O'Dette recordings of Dowland, I could narrow the search to those including both names. The better search engines allow the use of Boolean operators such as AND, OR, NOT, and so on to enable a more focused inquiry, usually with smaller and better results.

The query below produces a good list of reviews and listings of O'Dette recordings that include a Dowland work and information about the artist.

An AltaVista narrowing search

Harmonia Mundi's O'Dette page

Academic search resources are discussed in chapter 12.

YAHOO!

No discussion of searching the Web would be complete without mention of the Yahoo! catalog, currently the most famous and largest resource. A search here can discover Web pages of interest without the need of entering specific data.

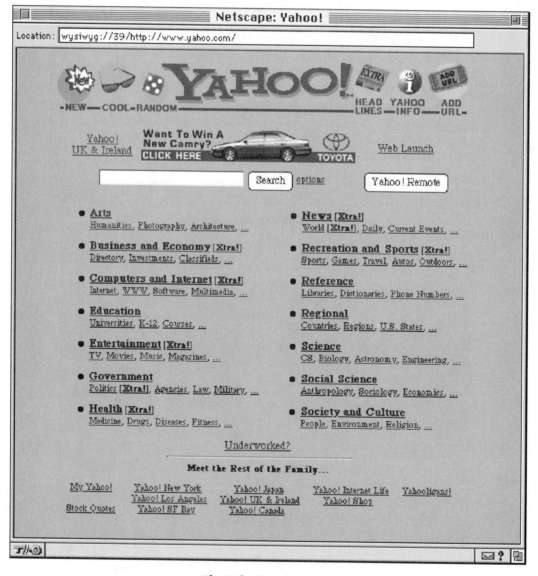

The Yahoo! main page

The layer-by-layer search method gets us through to a list of 161 guitar items.

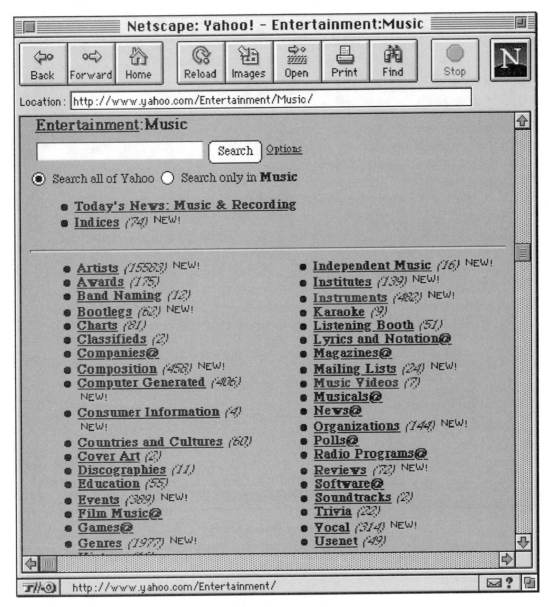

Yahoo!: Music listings

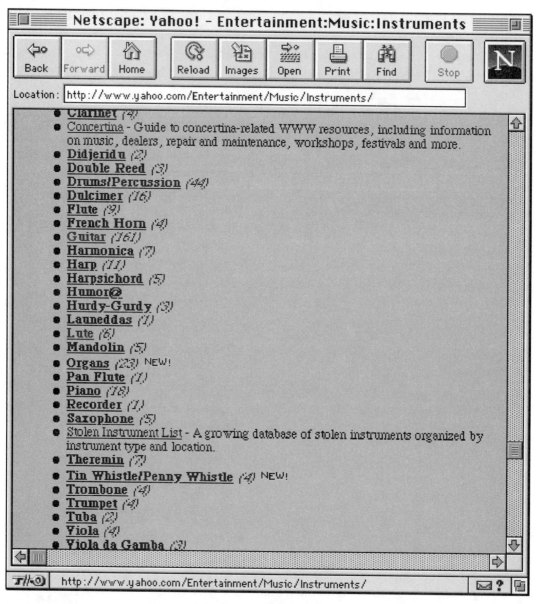

Yahoo!: Instrument listings

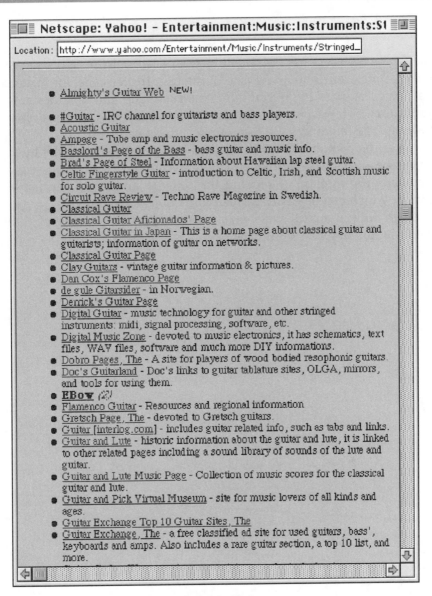

Yahoo!: Guitar listings

Typically you can work in closer and closer to your target. Having found it, you don't want to have to go through the whole hierarchy again, and here the solution is the *bookmark*.

BOOKMARKS

The better browsers have a simple way to keep a list of URLs so you can make a quick return to a Web site of interest. In Netscape, for instance, all that is necessary is to go to the Bookmarks menu and drag down to **Add Bookmark.** This saves a reference to the page that you are currently viewing. The references are listed under the same menu.

Later the bookmarks may be edited into orderly file folders by topic—very necessary as the number increases. Netscape makes this easy by a drag-and-drop method of moving the files up and down the list or into folders, which can be easily named with subject headings.

Searching is a skill well worth learning for the saving of time and faster finding of topics of interest.

TWELVE
MUSICOLOGY
ON THE INTERNET

It is hard to do specific research on the Internet at this time, though there is a wealth of material of general interest. For the guitarist interested in early music there is a fair amount of bibliographic information about lute, vihuela, and guitar tablatures, listed below. For now a good starting point is the home page of the American Musicological Society. This society also has a mailing list open to nonmembers by contacting **listproc@ucdavis.edu.**

Some of the direct links available from their page can be found on page 184.

The "Doctoral Dissertations in Musicology" link gives details of a project to have available information on the Web. The ability to find dissertations by subject grouping will be particularly useful. Further sources of dissertations and abstracts can be found on the "WWW Sites of Interest to Musicologists" link.

A rich source of on-line facilities is to be found under the heading "Music Libraries, Archives, and Online Catalogues," maintained by Mark Brill at the University of California, Davis. From these entries further entries may be found, and gradually you will form a large bookmark list in your browser tailored to your particular needs and interests.

Here are some places to explore for your bookmark list.

LIBRARIES

BLAISE: The British Library's Automated Information Service

http://portico.bl.uk/nbs/blaise/overview.html

BLAISE is an on-line information retrieval service that provides access to twenty-two databases containing over 17 million bibliographic records. The databases are accessed via a new user-friendly graphical interface on

Netscape: AMERICAN MUSICOLOGICAL SOCIETY

Back | Forward | Home | Reload | Images | Open | Print | Find | Stop

Location: http://musdra.ucdavis.edu/Documents/AMS/AMS.html

The **AMSLIST** is a discussion forum for musicology and issues related to musicology. It is open to anyone. Membership in the **AMS** is not required. To subscribe to the list, send a message to:

listproc@ucdavis.edu

with the following in the body of the message:

SUBSCRIBE AMSLIST [your first name] [your last name]

- AMS Directors
- Journal of the American Musicological Society
- AMS Committees
- AMS Chapter Officers
- Award and Fellowship Guidelines
- Calendar of Annual Meetings
- WWW Sites of Interest to Musicologists
- Forthcoming Conferences
- VIEWPOINT: The Musicological Job Market
- Doctoral Dissertations in Musicology

AMS WWW page maintained by Mark Brill
mebrill@ucdavis.edu
University of California-Davis
Last updated July 20, 1996

The American Musicological Society home page

the World Wide Web. A direct on-line link to the British Library Document Supply Centre, the world's leading supplier of documents, allows you to transmit requests for individual items quickly and easily.

COPAC

WWW:http://curlopac.ac.uk/curlinfo/

COPAC currently gives access to the combined university library catalogs of Cambridge, Edinburgh, Glasgow, Leeds, and Oxford. The catalogs of a further ten CURL member libraries will be added over the coming months. The service is still at an early stage of development but already provides search, retrieve, display, and download facilities via two interfaces, text and WWW. Access to COPAC is free of charge. User information is available at **http://copac.ac.uk/copacinfo/.**

Gesellschaft für Mathematik und Datenvararbeitung: Noten, CD

ftp://ftp.gmd.de/music/

Surprisingly, some actual music scores ready to print on a Postscript printer! Bach, Mozart, Corelli, and others.

Harvard University, Loeb Music Library

www.rism.harvard.edu/MusicLibrary/Welcome.html

Much interesting material, including the rare holdings of the Isham Memorial Collection. Harvard is also the U.S. home of RISM (see below).

Hytelnet Library Catalogues

http://library.usask.ca/hytelnet/sites1.htm

Maintained by Peter Scott, this site takes you rapidly to Telnet locations, with log-in or password instructions for each location. A great resource.

Indiana University Library

http://www.music.indiana.edu/muslib.html

As well as information on the resources of the William and Gayle Cook Music Library, this site covers access to important library catalogs for music in the United States and abroad, including libraries selected for the importance of their music collections. IU is a member of the Associated Music Libraries Group, a consortium of ten major U.S. music libraries. It includes direct links to the Library of Congress and BLAISE.

Infobahn Librarian

http://www.ualberta.ca/~nfriesen/

This site gives access to sources of interest to librarians as well as lists of libraries on the Net.

Italian Music Libraries

http://ICL382.CILEA.IT/music/mussigle.htm

A comprehensive list of Italian music libraries in alphabetical order.

The International Association of Music Information Centres IAMIC

http://www.ingress.com/amc/iamic.htm

The International Association of Music Information Centres has thirty-six members in thirty-two countries internationally. Each music information centre is responsible for documenting and promoting the music of its own country or region. Centres contain sheet music, sound archives, and biographical and research materials, and are open to the public.

International Federation of Library Associations and Institutions

http://www.nlc-bnc.ca/ifla/II/libdoc.htm

Many fascinating links relating to major projects are under way or planned. This is one to watch for information as digital library resources improve and expand.

The International Guitar Research Archive

http://www.csun.edu/~igra

This site is of particular interest to guitarists, concentrating on biographies, portraits, and music bibliography of famous guitar figures. CSUN (California State University, Northridge) is also the home of the Vahdah Olcott Bickford collection.

IRCAM

http://www.ircam.fr/index-e.html

A leading nonprofit organization, founded in 1977 by Pierre Boulez at the suggestion of President Georges Pompidou of France, IRCAM is considered by many the most advanced new music center in the world. The multimedia site reflects the high technology associated with the institute.

IRCAM Library

http://www.ircam.fr/biblio/query.html

An elaborate "Médiatèque" gives access to audio and video items as well as bibliographic information at this famous resource in Paris.

Libraries around the World

http://www.lib.utexas.edu/Libs/World_Libraries.html

Links to lists of libraries. Contains a direct link to the Library of Congress.

Library of Congress

gopher://marvel.loc.gov/11/global/arts/music

Access to the largest music library in the United States.

LIBWEB: Library WWW Services

http://sunsite.Berkeley.edu/libweb/

A comprehensive resource for finding links to libraries with Web pages.

Links to Music Information Projects (European Union)

http://www.echo.lu/libraries/en/music.html

An extensive list of links to current European music projects, international music associations, information sources by country, and much more.

Massachusetts Institute of Technology

http://nimrod.mit.edu/depts/music/music-top.html

The MIT Rosalind Denny Lewis Music Library, opened in 1996, houses reference and research materials including books, printed music, recordings, and periodicals.

The New York Public Library for the Performing Arts

http://gopher.nypl.org

Provides access to CATNYP, the on-line catalog of the research libraries of the New York Public Library.

RISM Series A/II Music Manuscripts

http://www.rism.harvard.edu/rism/Welcome.html#InternetProject

In February 1995 the RISM Zentralredaktion and the U.S. RISM office embarked on a joint development project with the aim of making the international RISM Series A/II Music Manuscripts Database available on line via the Internet.

RISM-US

http://www.sscm.harvard.edu/RISM/Welcome.html

RISM—the Répertoire International des Sources Musicales (International Inventory of Musical Sources)—represents a worldwide effort to identify and describe sources of music and writings about music from the earliest times through ca. 1825. The RISM home page is a joint production of the RISM Zentralredaktion in Frankfurt, Germany, and the U.S. RISM office at Harvard University.

Here is the description from the page itself: "The RISM WWW Home Page provides news and reports on RISM activities throughout the world, describes the various printed and on-line resources made available by the Zentral-redaktion and the U.S. RISM Office, and can help you gain access to them."

Sibelius Academy Music Resources

http://www.siba.fi/Kulttuuripalvelut/music.html

One of the most complete link lists, covering popular and folk music as well as classical, early music, and so on. Rated by *PC Magazine* as one of the top one hundred Web sites.

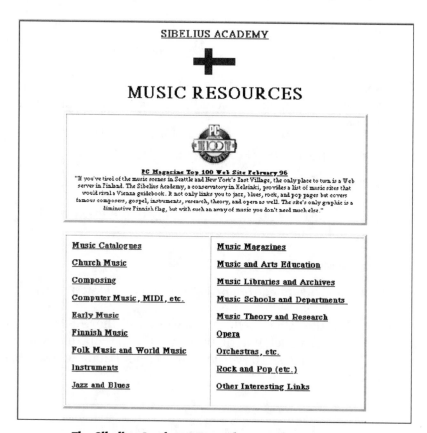

The Sibelius Academy: From the award-winning site

The Sonneck Society for American Music

http://www.aaln.org/sonneck

The Sonneck Society for American Music, a nonprofit scholarly and educational organization, seeks to stimulate the appreciation, performance, creation, and study of American music in all its historical and contemporary styles and contexts.

Thesaurus Musicarum Italicarum

http://candl.let.ruu.nl

The Department of Computer and Humanities at Utrecht University project to publish on CD-ROM a number of music treatises in Italian from the sixteenth and early seventeenth centuries. The first official publication (1997) is a CD of the treatises of Gioseffo Zarlino.

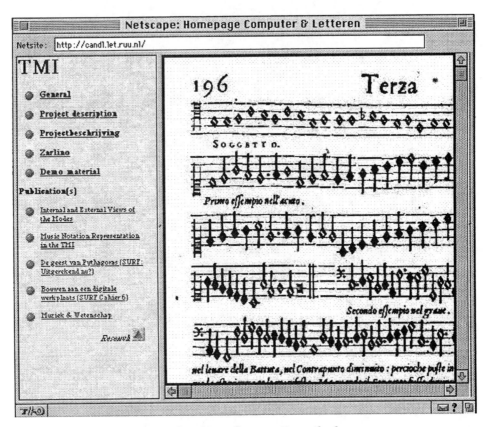

Thesaurus Musicarum Italicarum: From the home page

Thesaurus Musicarum Latinarum

gopher://iubvm.ucs.indiana.edu/11/tml

This database of music theory treatises in Latin from the Middle Ages and the early Renaissance can be found on a Gopher site from Indiana University. It contains both text and graphics and multiple versions where extant. A large and worthwhile project offering true content rather than just bibliography.

Salinas, De musica, *1r

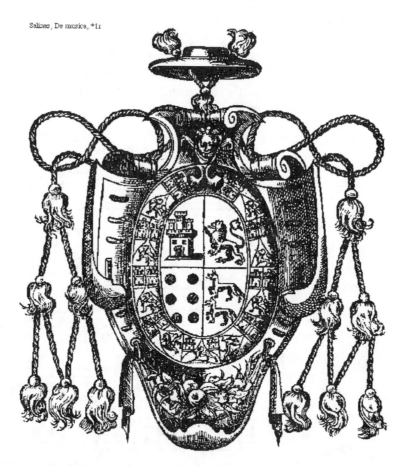

Thesaurus Musicarum Latina: Excerpt from Franciscus Salinas, *De musica* (1577)

University of North Texas

http://www.library.unt.edu/projects/lully/armprint.html

The illustration is from the Lully collection.

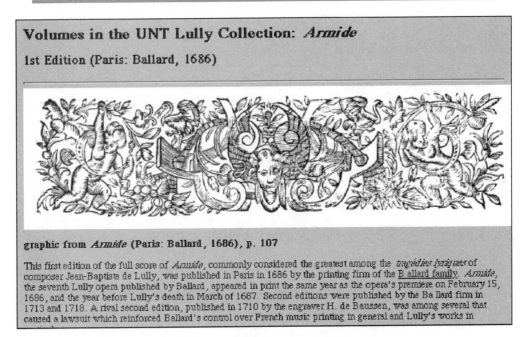

Volumes in the UNT Lully Collection: *Armide*

1st Edition (Paris: Ballard, 1686)

graphic from *Armide* (Paris: Ballard, 1686), p. 107

This first edition of the full score of *Armide*, commonly considered the greatest among the *tragédies lyriques* of composer Jean-Baptiste de Lully, was published in Paris in 1686 by the printing firm of the Ballard family. *Armide*, the seventh Lully opera published by Ballard, appeared in print the same year as the opera's premiere on February 15, 1686, and the year before Lully's death in March of 1687. Second editions were published by the Ballard firm in 1713 and 1718. A rival second edition, published in 1710 by the engraver H. de Baussen, was among several that caused a lawsuit which reinforced Ballard's control over French music printing in general and Lully's works in

Lully Project at the University of North Texas

Washington University in St. Louis, Gaylord Music Library

http://library.wustl.edu:80/~music

Home of the Krick guitar music collection.

Yale University

http://www.library.yale.edu/guide1.htm

Information on the many special collections, including the Beinecke Rare Book and Manuscript Library.

OPERA

English National Opera at the London Coliseum

http//:musicinfo.gold.ac.uk/opera/eno.html

Los Angeles Opera

http://www.primenet.com/~thoward/lamco/

La Scala

http://lascala.milano.it

New York City Opera

http://www.interport.net/~nycopera/

The Opera-L Home Page in France

http://pf1pn7.ill.fr/html/opera-l/opera-l.html

The Royal Opera House, Covent Garden

http://musicinfo.gold.ac.uk/opera/roh.html

The Royal Swedish Opera House

http://www3.ios.com:80/~gberkson/operan/index.html

Salzburger Festspiele

hirsch.cosy.sbg.ac.at/kultur/salzfest95/efestspiel.html

Santa Fe Opera

www.walpole.com/walpole/Santa_Fe_Opera

Wiener Staatsoper, Wiener Volksoper

www.austria-info.at/kultur/ws-wv/

EARLY MUSIC

Early Music America

http://www.cwru.edu/orgs/ema/

Early Music Archives

gopher://olymp.wu-wien.ac.at/11/.earlym-l

Early Music WWW

www.virtual.com/jr/earlym.html

Early Music and SCORE Archive (Acadia University, Canada)

ace.acadiau.ca/dat/ftp/music

Hildegard of Bingen (1) (UCSB)

http://tweedledee.ucsb.edu/~kris/music/Hildegard.html

Journal of Seventeenth-Century Music (Harvard)

www.sscm.harvard.edu/jscm/Welcome.html

The Lute Society of America

http://www.cs.dartmouth.edu/~wbc/lsa/lsa.html

Sixteenth-Century Printed Tablatures for the Lute, Vihuela, Guitar, and Cittern

http://www.lib.duke.edu/music/lute/home.html

A comprehensive list compiled by Dr. Gary R. Boye, with explanations of how to interpret the various tablature forms. He states, "This is an ongoing project; eventually, each book will be analyzed as to contents, and individual incipits of the pieces (in tablature) will be placed in a searchable thematic catalogue."

Renaissance Consort

http://www.hike.te.chiba-u.ac.jp/cons1/

Renaissance Instruments

http://www.hike.te.chiba-u.ac.jp/cons1/

Society for Seventeenth-Century Music

http://rism.harvard.edu/sscm/

The Galpin Society for the Study of Musical Instruments

http://www.music.ed.ac.uk/euchmi/galpin/index.html#gw

Publishers of the *Galpin Society Journal.*

Vatican Exhibit: Early Manuscripts

http://www.ncsa.uiuc.edu/SDG/Experimental/vatican.exhibit/exhibit/e-music/Music.html

Classical Composers (1000): Picture Gallery

http://spight.physics.unlv.edu/picgalr2.html

Internet Resources for Composers

http://kahless.isca.uiowa.edu/~kcorey/sci/resources.html

Purcell Page

http://www.voicenet.com/~hohmann/purcell/index.html

Scarlatti Keyboard Works (Eindhoven University of Technology, Netherlands)

http://www.win.tue.nl/scarlatti

This is an amazing resource, not to be missed!

Heitor Villa-Lobos

http://www.ibase.org.br/~mvillalobos

Access to the Villa-Lobos museum in Brazil is illustrated in chapter eight above.

COMPUTER MUSIC

The Center for Computer Research in Music and Acoustics (CCRMA)

http://ccrma-www.stanford.edu

The Stanford University Center for Computer Research in Music and Acoustics (CCRMA) is a multidisciplinary facility where composers and researchers work together using computer-based technology both as an artistic medium and as a research tool.

The Classical MIDI Connection

http://www.dtx.net/~raborn/

MIDI Home Page

http://www.eeb.ele.tue.nl/midi/index.html

Contains descriptions, prices, and so on.

Music Instruction Software

http://www.cstp.umkc.edu/users/bhugh/musici.html

MUSIC PUBLISHING

Music Publishers' Association of the United States

http://host.mpa.org/mpa/Welcome.html

BMG Classical Music World

http://classicalmus.com

Classical Links around the Web

http://www.demon.co.uk/creative/fairfiel/classics.html

Internet Resources for Music Scholars

http://www.rism.harvard.edu/MusicLibrary/InternetResources.html

MIDI Connection File Library: Renaissance Period

http://mail.dtx-bbs.com/~raborn/renaissa.html

Music Newsgroups and Listservs

http://www.music.fsu.edu/news.html

Music Research Information System (MRIS)

gopher://runner.utsa.edu:3000/

Music Resources on the Internet (Indiana University)

http://www.music.indiana.edu/misc/music_resources.htm

Selected Web Resources for Music and Musicology (Princeton University)

http://www.princeton.edu:80/~stmoore/musiclinks.html

Music FTP Sites

http://gps.leeds.ac.uk/music/NetInfo/MusicFTP/ftp_sites.html

Copyright Information

http://www.benedict.com/register.htm#register

GOING ON
FROM HERE

COMPOSING AND SCORING

The role of the computer in the world of music will undoubtedly increase in the years to come. In the area of composition and scoring one can only hope that the trend will be toward greater simplicity of interface, and perhaps with more facilities for those musicians concerned with live music rather than MIDI. One complex program mentions having the capacity to handle one hundred voices; anyone who has tried writing even eight-part counterpoint will find this daunting rather than appealing. In truth, it takes careful planning and programming to achieve simplicity, and one of the dangers of the perceived need to upgrade constantly with new features and new documentation is in fact a lessening of general usability. Musicians who are not in the MIDI world do not *need* computers, just as authors do not in fact need word processors. But if something can be found to assist what would otherwise be a chore (such as writing out parts), then it has a value. It is also true to say that some operations may take longer with a computer but may in fact be more enjoyable, and this is also a valid justification for their use.

RECORDING

As the price and availability of large storage devices improve—and that improvement is currently happening on an almost daily basis—the practicality of home recording and editing increases. The skills required are considerable, however, and as stated above, my view is that digital recording is better left to professionals. They will probably continue to use dedicated hardware for recording and editing, and no doubt the hardware and

196

software will improve as digital recording becomes the norm. For home use computers may be used, but for now a conventional tape recorder is simpler.

CD-ROMS

The CD-ROM has not yet proved itself an inevitable asset to the musician. There are huge catalogs in this form issued by libraries, but their cost puts them out of the range of the amateur. Much of what was projected for CD-ROMs, apart from the simple storage of computer programs, will probably find its way onto the Internet. People hate to wait for information while wheels crank and grind, and CD-ROMs are still comparatively slow of access. The Internet, by contrast, becomes faster and more accessible by the day.

THE INTERNET

The continuation of the phenomenal growth of the Internet is inevitable. As pages proliferate, however, the problems of selection increase, making the role of the search engine ever more important. These engines must become the library reference desks of the future, and catalogs of sites will grow daily in importance. One of the problems is that the Internet is organized in pages rather than in volumes, so each user must in effect make up his or her own books as well as bookmarks. More than one music historian has gone on record to discredit the Internet as a tool of serious research. Roaming the Net can be quite as time-consuming as visiting a good library, and certainly at this time the resources on the Net are minuscule by comparison. Nevertheless, there are some interesting resources to be found, and ambitious plans are going ahead to improve the availability of true content. After many hours of wandering from reference to reference through the Internet, the average musician might well feel that there is only "information about information" rather than actual material to enjoy or study. There is a reason, of course: it takes a lot of work to present material on the Net, since even simple text needs to be converted to HTML and either typed or scanned into computer files. Then a server with a connection to the Internet must be employed to present the information round the clock, and that server in turn has connection fees and power bills to pay as well as staff for technical support and maintenance. All of this adds up to a bill for benevolence if the material is to be presented free of charge. Of course, offerings may be made with a modest fee attached, but at the time of this writing a truly satisfactory and secure way to pay for Internet merchandise has not been developed. Because computer hackers can easily access E-mail and in fact can usually break so-called secure systems in a day or two, an order must still be called in by telephone or arrangements made to establish an account by conventional means. The end result is that valuable content will be provided only where there is charitable, academic, or government funding, or where a satisfactory pay method is available and patronized.

Under the charitable heading may be included individual enthusiasts willing to share their hobby interests with others, but such sources tend to be slender in content as the original urge to share gives way to an appreciation of the labor involved. Fortunately, some foundations with extensive resources have chosen to support this form of outlet. One of the first and best of these is Project Gutenberg, which aims to make more than ten thousand books and other documents available electronically by the year 2001. Begun in 1991, the project already maintains a library of hundreds of books and stories, from Aesop's Fables to *Through the Looking Glass,* which can be freely downloaded. In the music field it is to be hoped that some of the monumental works of the past may find their way onto the Internet through similar dedicated volunteers. These projects are Herculean tasks and will take time. But the benefit is that the process is cumulative even if we are only at the first step of the thousand-mile journey.

Audio on the Internet

It is naturally of interest to the musician to learn that there is audio capability on the Internet. Two main types are currently in use. One is a file that must first be downloaded; if it is a digital audio file, this means a tedious wait for the file to arrive. Digital files are very large, and even a thirty-second clip takes minutes to arrive. When it does, the browser starts up a playback program that places a small control panel on the screen so the music may be repeated if desired. Sometimes the sampling rate, and hence quality, is reduced to make the file smaller, but the results are rarely worth the trouble of downloading.

MIDI files fare better, since they are small and therefore quick to download. Here also most modern browsers are equipped to play the files automatically. For an interesting example of this type of audio it is worth a visit to the Scarlatti site at **http://cursus14.win.tue.nl:4321/scarlatti.** A huge resource of MIDI files of Scarlatti sonatas (here called exercises) may be played with virtually no delay at startup.

More interesting than files that have to be downloaded is the second main type of audio, known as *streaming audio.* Here the object is to present a continuous "broadcast" to the user. The technology is improving rapidly, and the software to play the audio stream may be freely downloaded. An example of such a site is at **http://www.realaudio.com/products/ra3.0/launch.ram,** where a free player can be obtained and samples heard. KING-FM of Seattle can be heard broadcasting classical music live on the Internet twenty-four hours a day, seven days a week.

The audio quality is remarkably good considering the technical complexities involved. Unfortunately, there is a drawback—at busy times on the Internet there is the occasional sudden silence, which can be disconcerting. Nevertheless, the technique is remarkable and conjures up amazing visions of hundreds or thousands of stations broadcasting from around the world. A station I heard broadcasting from Thailand on the Internet had similar quality to the Seattle station.

"Live" Video on the Internet

The technique for video is not yet as successful as that for audio transmission. Small pictures can be received, but these appear more like fast-moving slide shows. At this time video reception may be considered an area for hobbyists, not yet of much significance to the world of music.

FURTHER READING

For an in-depth study of computers and music, Chris Yavelow's monumental *Macworld Music and Sound Bible* (San Mateo, CA: IDG Books Worldwide, 1992) is a must for the Macintosh user. A composer, Yavelow had to condense some of his encyclopedic knowledge to make it fit into the nearly fourteen hundred pages of the first edition.

Experiencing Music Technology by David Brian Williams and Peter Richard Webster (New York: Schirmer Books, 1996) offers an extensive university-level course on the subject and is not confined to a particular platform.

For the beginning enthusiast, an excellent magazine, *Music and Computers* (bimonthly; San Francisco: Miller Freeman), is skillfully informative without talking down to the neophyte or becoming overtechnical.

Internet books abound, but for reference *Harley Hahn's Internet and Web Yellow Pages* (Berkeley, CA: Osborne/McGraw-Hill, 1997) will be found valuable. Unfortunately, Internet addresses change frequently, so it is important to get the latest edition. Another source of many music URLs is *The Virtual Musician* by Brad Hill (New York: Schirmer Books, 1996).

This is a small survey of a huge topic, but my hope is that it will have helped some musicians to decide whether for them the computer is worthy of further exploration.

APPENDIX
MUSIC NOTATION PROGRAMS

The list presented here derives from a compilation originally undertaken for the Internet by Dennis O'Neill in response to frequently asked questions.

While every effort has been made to update and add to the list, so many new programs as well as upgrades of existing software appear that it is impossible to be truly current and complete. However, many manufacturers now have Web pages so up-to-date pricing and innovations may be simply accessed.

List prices are not always charged at the retail level where "street prices" prevail, and reductions or special prices (e.g., for teachers and students) are sometimes made by the manufacturer. Thus it is always worth making enquiries before ruling out software just because of price.

It cannot be too strongly emphasized that "try before you buy" should be the watchword wherever possible.

Here is the structure of individual entries:

Name:	**Name of the software**
Platforms:	What computer(s) may be used
Requirements:	Minimum requirements, such as memory, model etc.
List price:	List price
Manufacturer:	Person or company that produces the software
Demo:	Where to get a demo if available
Review:	If known, where to find a review of this application
To acquire:	Where to buy if no entry order from manufacturer
Sound output:	Whether this software will play the music a user has entered
Notes:	Any special comments

PROGRAM INFORMATION LISTING

Name: **abc2mtex version 1.6.1**

Platforms:	Any system supporting MusicTeX and TeX
Requirements:	TeX/LaTeX and MusicTeX
Price:	Free
Manufacturer:	Chris Walshaw < C.Walshaw@gre.ac.uk >
Demo:	None (it's free—get the distribution)
To acquire:	http://www.gre.ac.uk/~ c.walshaw/abc
Sound output:	MIDI

Name: **ACCU Music System version 3.7**

Platforms:	MS-DOS, OS/2
Requirements:	Any 80x86, 384kb RAM, MS-DOS 3.3 or higher
Price:	Shareware: $20 plus $3 shipping (U.S.) or $6 (other countries). This is nagware, i.e., it displays a message asking the user to register.
Manufacturer:	Kevin Fischer (kfischer@seas.ucla.edu) c/o ACCU Music System 16878 Saint James Drive Poway, CA 92064-1137
To acquire:	MS-DOS ftp://oak.oakland.edu/Simtelnet/msdos/music/ac37musd.zip

Name: **Bucket o' tab (music tablature)**

Platforms:	Windows 3.1, Win95
Requirements:	VBRUN300.DLL (available at the BOT web site)ftp://ocsystems.com/pub/gse/vbrun300.zip
List price:	$25 (shareware)
Manufacturer:	Scott Evans PO Box 316 Oakton, VA 22124 gse@his.com
Demo:	None (it's shareware—get the whole package)
To acquire:	ftp://ocsystems.com/pub/gse/bucket.zip (see README file)
Sound output:	MIDI

Name: **CMN (Common Music Notation)**

Platforms:	NeXT, Mac, SGI, Linux

Requirements:	Common Lisp; CLOS (pcl); PostScript; Sonata or Petrucci font
List price:	Free
Manufacturer:	Bill Schottstaedt (bil@ccrma.stanford.edu).
Demo:	None (freeware)
Review:	
To acquire:	ftp://ccrma-ftp.stanford.edu/pub/Lisp/cmn.tar.gz
	ftp://ccrma-ftp.stanford.edu/pub/Lisp/cmn.README

Name:	**The Composer's Pen**
Platforms:	MS-DOS, Amstrad PCW
Requirements:	DOS 3, 512KB RAM, 8086, EGA, CGA, VGA, Hercules
List price:	£150 UK
Manufacturer:	Composit Software
	10 Leasowe Green
	Lightmoor, Telford, Shropshire, England TF4 3QX
	(44) 952 595 436
Review:	*Keyboard* (December 1994): 69ff.
Sound output:	No

Name:	**Composer's WorkBench**
Platforms:	(MS-DOS) the current fuly supported version is for Linux operating system
Requirements:	80386 or better, 640X480 pixel resolution graphics adapter or better, Linux OS, Roland MPU-401 or compatible MIDI card, MIDI synth.
List price:	$50 plus shipping (shareware)
Manufacturer:	Dennis McNamara (dmcnamar@netcom.com)
Demo:	None (shareware)
Review:	
To acquire:	ftp://oak.oakland.edu/SimTelnet/ msdos/music/cwb135.zip
Sound output:	MIDI

Name:	**ConcertWare Home CD**
Platforms:	Mac, MS-Windows
Requirements:	Mac: System 7, 2 MB, 68020
	PC: MS-Windows 3.1, 2 MB, 386, SoundBlaster compatible
List price:	$39.99
Manufacturer:	Jump Software
	201 San Antonio Circle, Suite 172

	Mountain View, CA 94040
	415-917-7460, 415-917-7490 (fax)
	http://www.jumpmusic.com
Demo:	None
Review:	*Keyboard* (December 1994): 69ff.
To acquire:	Software and music stores and web page
Sound output:	Any MIDI interface (PC: Windows MPC)

Name:	**Cubasis Audio (PC)**
	Cubasis AV (Mac)
Platforms:	Mac, PC
	Windows 95
Requirements:	Power Mac: 601,604, or 604E
	RAM: 16 MG (Min), 32 MB recommended
	PC: Pentium 90 running Windows 95
	16 MB Ram
	Windows Sound card
List price:	$149
Manufacturer:	Steinberg
	17700 Raymer St., Suite 1001
	Northridge, CA 91325
	818-993-4091, 818-701-7452 (fax)
Demo:	http://www.Steinberg.net
To acquire:	Music and software stores or manufacturer
Sound output:	MIDI or digital audio

Name:	**Cubase Score VST**
Platforms:	Mac, PC
Requirements:	Mac: System 7, 4MB RAM
	PC: at least Pentium/166mhz
List price:	$549
Manufacturer:	Steinberg
	17700 Raymer St., Suite 1001
	Northridge, CA 91325
	818-993-4091, 818-701-7452 (fax)
Demo:	http://www.Steinberg.net
Review	*Electronic Musician* (July 1993)
To acquire:	
Sound output:	Mac: any MIDI interface; PC: MPU-401 compatible

Name:	**Encore**
Platforms:	Mac, MS-Windows

Requirements: Mac: 4MB, 16MHz
                   PC: Windows 3.1, 4MB, 16 MHz, MPU 404, VGA or
                   better
List price: $599
Manufacturer: Passport Designs, Inc.
                   100 Stone Pine Road
                   Half Moon Bay, CA 94019
                   415-726-0280, 415-726-2254 (fax)
Demo: http://www.passportdesigns.com
Review: Alan Belkin, "Macintosh Notation Software: Present
                   and Future," *Computer Music Journal* 18, no. 1
                   (Spring 1994)
                   Electronic Musician (April 1994)
To acquire: Software stores, music stores, or web site
Sound output: Any MIDI interface, sound card

Name: **Finale**

Platforms: Mac, MS-Windows
Requirements: Mac: MAc Plus or better
                   System 6.0.7 with 4MB or better
                   System 7.5 requires 8 MB RAM
                   Power Mac: 6100 or better, System 7.1.2 or
                   higher, 8 MB RAM
                   PC: 386 or higher, 4MB RAM
                   Windows 3.1 or better
List price: $545; $275 for academicians and students
Manufacturer: Coda Music Technology
                   6210 Bury Dr.
                   Eden Prairie, MN 55346-1718
                   800-843-2066, 612-937-9760 (fax)
Demo: http:///www.codamusic.com
Review: Alan Belkin, "Macintosh Notation Software: Present
                   and Future," *Computer Music Journal* 18, no. 1
                   (Spring 1994)
                   Electronic Musician (December 1993)
To acquire: Software stores, music stores
Sound output: MIDI/sound card

Name: **Finale Allegro**

Platforms: Mac, MS-Windows
Requirements: Mac: Mac Plus or better
                   System 6.0.7 or newer, 4MB RAM

System 7 required for balloon help and TrueType fonts
PC: Minimum 386 with 4 MB RAM, 486 w/8 MB recommended
Windows 3.1 or better

List price:	$199
Manufacturer:	Coda Music Technology
	6210 Bury Dr.
	Eden Prairie, MN 55346-1718
	800-843-2066, 612-937-9760 (fax)
Demo:	http:///www.codamusic.com
Review:	*Electronic Musician* (April 1994)
To acquire:	Software stores, music stores
Sound output:	MIDI/sound card

Name:	**Fronimo (Lute Tablature)**
Platforms:	Windows
Requirements:	Windows 3.1,95,NT
List price:	$100 + $10 shipping
Manufacturer:	Francesco Triboli tribioli@arcetri.astro.it
Demo:	ftp://sisifo.arcetri.astro.it/pub/fronimo/fronimo.zip
To acquire:	Francesco Tribioli
	Via di Mezzana 21
	50065 Pontassieve (FI)
	Italy
Sound output:	MIDI

Name:	**Laser Music Processor**
Platforms:	PC
Requirements:	DOS 2.1 or better, 640KB, 8086-4.77, graphics
	Runs under Windows 95 without MIDI
List price:	$30 plus shipping
Manufacturer:	Teach Services
	Donovan Rd., Route 1, Box 182
	Brushton, NY 12916
	518-358-2125, 518-358-3028 (fax)
Demo:	None
Review:	*Keyboard* (December 1994): 69ff
Sound output:	Any MIDI interface

Name:	**Lime**
Platforms:	Mac, MS-Windows
Requirements:	Mac: 68030 or better, System 7 or greater

	8MB RAM, 16 recommended 020
	PC: Windows 95 and NT, 12MB RAM, 386 or better, VGA
List price:	$295
Manufacturer:	Lippold Haken and Dorothea Blostein
	Electronic Courseware Systems
	1210 Lancaster Dr.
	Champaign, IL 61821
	800-832-4965, 217-359-7099
Demo:	http://www.ecsmedia.com
Review:	Alan Belkin, "Macintosh Notation Software: Present and Future," *Computer Music Journal* 18, no. 1 (Spring 1994)
	Electronic Musician (April 1994)
To acquire:	Music and software stores or manufacturer
Sound output:	MIDI interface

Name:	**Logic**
Platforms:	Mac, PC
Requirements:	Mac: 040 processor or better, System 7 or better, 8 MB RAM
	PC: 486 or better, Windows 3.1 or better, 8 MB RAM
List price:	Mac: 449
	PC: $399
Manufacturer:	Emagic, Inc.
	13348 Grass Valley Ave.
	Building C, Suite 100
	Grass Valley, CA 95945
	916-477-1051, etx. 12
	http://www.emagic.de
Demo	Go to web site
Review:	*Keyboard* (December 1994): 69ff
To acquire	Music or software stores
Sound output:	Any MIDI interface

Name:	**Logic Audio**
Platforms:	Mac, PC
Requirements:	Mac: 040/180mhz or faster, System 7 or better, 16MB RAM, 32 MB recommended
	PC: 486/66mhz minimum, Pentium recommended Windows 95, 16 MB RAM
List price:	Mac $799

	PC $699
Manufacturer:	Emagic, Inc.
	13348 Grass Valley Ave
	Building C, Suite 100
	Grass Valley, CA 95945
	916-477-1051, etx. 12
	http://www.emagic.de
Demo:	Go to web site
Review:	*Keyboard* (December 1994): 69ff
To acquire:	Music and software stores
Sound output:	Any MIDI interface

Name:	**Melody Master**
Platforms:	MS-DOS
Requirements:	440 KB to install
List price:	$19 plus $4 shipping, $49 plus $4 shipping for commercial users (shareware)
Manufacturer:	Alexei A. Efros Jr.
To acquire:	ftp://oak.oakland.edu/SimTelnet/msdos/music/melody26.zip

Name:	**MicroLogic**
Platforms:	Mac,Windows
Requirements:	Mac: system 6.0.5, 4MB RAM, 040 or better
	PC: Windows 3.1, 4 MB RAM, 486 or better, 8 MB RAM
List price:	$99
Manufacturer:	Emagic, Inc.
	13348 Grass Valley Ave
	Building C, Suite 100
	Grass Valley, CA 95945
	916-477-1051, etx. 12
	http://www.emagic.de
Demo:	Go to web site
To acquire:	Music or software stores
Review:	*Keyboard* (December 1994): 69ff
Sound output:	MIDI

Name:	**MIDI Orchestrator Plus**
Platforms:	MS-Windows
Requirements:	Windows 3.1, 4MB, 386SX-20, VGA
List price:	$129.95
Manufacturer:	Voyetra Technologies

5 Odell Plaza
Yonkers, NY 10701
914-966-0600, 914-966-1102 (fax)

Demo:	http://www.voyetra.com
Review:	*Keyboard* (December 1994): 69ff
Sound output:	Any MIDI with Windows driver

Name: **MIDISCAN**

Platforms:	MS-Windows
Requirements:	386 or better, Windows 3.1 or better, digital scanner. Minimum 4 MB RAM, 8 MB recommended
List price:	$299
Manufacturer:	Musitek
	410 Bryant Circle, Suite K
	Ojai, CA 93023
	800-676-8055, 805-646-8099 (fax)
Review	*Computer Shopper* (February 1995)
Sound output:	MIDI
Notes:	Scans sheet music into Type I MIDI files.

Name: **Mosaic (formerly Composer's Mosaic)**

Platforms:	Mac
Requirements:	System 7.1 or less, 8MB RAM
	System 7.5 or better, 12MB RAM
	Power Mac, 16MB RAM
List price:	$595 list price
	Competitive upgrade from other product, $195
Manufacturer:	Mark of the Unicorn
	1280 Massachusetts Ave.
	Cambridge, MA 02138
	617-576-2760, 617-576-3609 (fax)
Demo:	http://www.motu.com
	(demo of the previous version)
Review:	Alan Belkin, "Macintosh Notation Software: Present and Future," *Computer Music Journal* 18, no. 1 (Spring 1994)
	Keyboard, February 1993
To acquire:	Music and software stores or through manufacturer
Sound output:	Any MIDI interface

Name: **Mozart**

Platforms:	MS-Windows

Requirements: MS-Windows, at least 486 recommended
List price: $49 shareware registration
Manufacturer: Dave Webber (dave@musical.demon.co.uk)
Demo: None (shareware; get the distribution)
Review:
To acquire: http://www.mozart.co.uk/programs/mozart.zip
   or: ftp://ftp.simtelnet/pub/simtelnet/win3/music/
                  mozart20.zip
                  The zip file includes two versions of MOZART:
                  MOZART 1.4 for Windows 3.1 and MOZART 2.0 for
                  Windows 95. When you run the setup program the
                  correct one installs automatically according to your
                  operating system.

Name: **MUSE**

Platforms: Windows 95 or Windows NT
Requirements: Windows 95 or Windows NT
List price: £10 UK, $15 U.S., $20 Australian
Manufacturer: Musements < laurie.griffiths@ukonline.co.uk >
Demo: Download it and get 30-day free trial
To acquire: http://web.ukonline.co.uk/members/laurie.griffiths
Sound Output: MIDI

Name: **Musicator Win 2.0**

Platforms: MS-Windows
Requirements: Windows 3.1 or better, M 8 mg audio 164 MB
List price: $299/399
Manufacturer: Musicator
                   PO BOX 73793
                   Davis, CA 95617
                   916-759-9424, 916-756-9807 (tech support)
Demo: www.musicator.com
Review: *Keyboard* (December 1994): 69ff
To acquire: Computer and music stores
Sound output: Windows MCI MIDI output (to sound card, MIDI interface)

Name: **Musicator Audio**

Platforms: MS-Windows
Requirements: Windows 3.1 or better, 16MB RAM
List price: $399
Manufacturer: Musicator
                   PO BOX 73793

Davis CA, 95617
916-759-9424, 916-756-9807 (tech support)
To acquire: Computer and music stores
Sound output: MIDI and Digital Audio

Haven't contacted, no evidence on-line

Name: **Music Pad**

Platforms: MS-DOS, Amstrad PCW
Requirements: DOS 3, 512KB RAM, 8086
List price: £19.95 UK
Manufacturer: Composit Software
                       10 Leasowe Green
                       Lightmoor, Telford, Shropshire, England TF4 3QX
                       (44)952 595 436
Review: *Keyboard* (December 1994): 69ff
Sound output: No

Name: **MusicPrinter Plus**

Platforms: MS-DOS
Requirements: DOS 2.0, 640KB, 10MHz, graphics
List price: $495; $295 for academicians and students
Manufacturer: Temporal Acuity Products, Inc.
                       Bld. #1, Suite 200
                       300 120th Ave. NE
                       Bellevue, WA 98005
                       800-426-2673, 206-462-1007, 206-462-1057 (fax)
Demo: ftp://celtic.stanford.edu/pub/tunes/Music.Printer
                       (several files) or call manufacturer
To acquire: Software stores, music stores, or manufacturer
Review: *Keyboard* (December 1994): 69ff
Sound output: Any MIDI interface

Name: **Musicshop**

Platforms: Mac, MS-Windows
Requirements: PC: 486 or better with 12MB RAM
                       Sound card
                       Windows 3.1 or Windows 95
List price: $119.95
Manufacturer: Opcode Systems, Inc.
                       3950 Fabian Way

	Palo Alto, CA 94303
	415-856-3333
Review:	*Electronic Musician* (September 1993)
	Keyboard (October 1993)
To acquire:	Music and Software stores
Sound output:	MIDI, Sound card

Name:	**MusicTime**
Platforms:	Mac, MS-Windows
Requirements:	Mac: Mac Classic II or better, System 7 or better
	4MB RAM Built in synthesizer requires Quicktime 2.0
	(included) and a 68020 processor
	PC: 486DX-66 or better, Pentium 120 recommended
	8 MB RAm, 16 MB recommended
	Windows compatible sound card Windows 3.1 or
	Windows 95, 4MB, 16 MHz, VGA or better
List price:	$99
Manufacturer:	Passport Designs, Inc.
	100 Stone Pine Road,
	Half Moon Bay, CA 94019
	415-726-0280, 415-726-2254 (fax)
Demo:	http://www.passportdesigns.com
To acquire:	Software stores, music stores
Sound output:	Any MIDI interface, sound card

Name:	**Nightingale**
Platforms:	Mac
Requirements:	System 6.0.5, 2MB; System 7, 3MB
List price:	$495; $295 for academicians and students
Manufacturer:	Temporal Acuity Products
	300 120th Ave. NE, Bldg. 1
	Bellevue, WA 98005
	800-426-2673, 206-462-1007, 206-462-1057 (fax)
Demo:	Free demo disk available on request
Review:	Alan Belkin, "Macintosh Notation Software: Present and Future," *Computer Music Journal* 18, no. 1 (Spring 1994)
	Electronic Musician (May 1994)
	Keyboard (April 1994)
To acquire:	Software stores, music stores, or manufacturer
Sound output:	Any MIDI interface

Name: **NoteScan**

Platforms: Mac
List price: $149.95
Notes: Music OCR add-on sold with Nightingale (see above)

Name: **NoteWorthy Composer 1.3.1B**

Platforms: MS-Windows
Requirements:
List price: Shareware: £40 UK, $39 in U.S.
Manufacturer: Braeburn Software
     Hawthorn Bank
     Scott's Place
     Selkirk, Scotland TD7 4DP
     Telephone 01750-721854
     Contact in U.S.: NoteWorthy ArtWare
     9432 Jenmar Dr.
     Fuquay-Varina, NC 27526-9647
Review: *PC Plus* (June 1994)
     UK Computer Shopper (April 1993)
To Acquire: ftp://oak.oakland.edu/SimTelnet/win3/music/
     nwc131B.zip
Sound output: Sound card or MIDI port

Name: **NoteWriter**

Platforms: Mac
Requirements: Mac Plus or better
List price: $295, $20 System 7 upgrade for registered users
Manufacturer: Opus 1 Music Inc.,
     499 E 37th Ave.
     Vancouver, B.C., Canada V5W 1E8
Review: Craig Weston, "NoteWriter: a Unique Approach to
     Music Printing Software," *Musicus* 2/i & ii
     (June/December 1990): 121–32

Name: **Overture**

Platforms: Mac
Requirements: 68020 or better, System 7, 2 MB
List price: $495
Manufacturer: Opcode Systems
     3950 Fabian Way, Suite 100
     Palo Alto, CA 94303

	415-494-1112, 415-856-3332 fax
To acquire:	Music stores, software stores
Review:	*Keyboard* (December 1994): 69ff
Sound output:	Any MIDI interface

Name:	**QuickScore Professional**
Platforms:	MS-Windows
Requirements:	Windows 3.1, 4MB RAM, 386-33, VGA
List price:	$79.95
Manufacturer:	Sion Software
	4497 W. 6th Ave
	Vancouver, B.C., Canada, VGR 1V2
	604/222-2454
	http://www.infoserve.net/quickscore
To acquire:	Manufacturer, software stores, music stores
Review:	*Keyboard* (December 1994): 69ff
Sound output:	MPU compatible, most sound cards

Name:	**Rhapsody 3**
Platforms:	Acorn & NCOS based Network Computers
Requirements:	2MB & RISC OS 3.1
List price:	£99.95 UK
Manufacturer:	Clares
	98 Middlewich Road
	Rudheath, Northwich
	Cheshire CW9 7DA United Kingdom
	Telephone: (UK access code, then) +44 606 48 511
	E-mail: dclare@clares.demon.co.uk
Demo:	Yes
To acquire:	Credit card or UK cheque
Sound output:	Internal or via MIDI

Name:	**Score**
Platforms:	PC, NeXT under SoftPC
Requirements:	DOS 3.2, 1MB, 80286, CGA to VGA, Hercules
List price:	$825
Manufacturer:	San Andreas Press (Leland Smith)
	P.O. Box 60247
	Palo Alto, CA 94306
	415-856-9394
Demo:	ftp://acc.acaiau.ca/dat/ftp/music
Sound output:	MPU-401 compatible

Name:	**Sibelius 7**
Platforms:	Acorn Archimedes, Acorn RISC PC
Requirements:	1 MB
List price:	$1499 U.S., £795 UK
Manufacturer:	Sibelius Software
	75 Burleigh St.
	Cambridge CB1 1DJ United Kingdom
	Telephone: (int'l access, then) 44 1223 302 765
	Fax: (int'l access, then) 44 1223 351 947
	U.S. branch:
	8000 Venice Blvd., Ste. 216
	Los Angeles, CA 90034
	Telephone 888-4-SIBELIUS
Review:	*Keyboard* (December 1994): 69ff
Sound output:	MIDI
Notes:	U.S. office also representatives for the Acorn computer

Name:	**SongWright**
Platforms:	MS-DOS
Requirements:	DOS 2.1 or better, 512KB, CGA EGA VGA
List price:	$99.95
Manufacturer:	SongWright Software
	7 Loudoun St., S.E.
	Leesburg, Va. 22075
	703-777-7232, 800-877-8070 (orders)
Demo:	30-day money-back guarantee
Review:	*Keyboard* (December 1994): 69ff
Sound output:	MPU-401 compatible, SoundBlaster

Name:	**SpeedScore**
Platforms:	Mac
Requirements:	68030 or better, Power Mac
List price:	$89.95
Manufacturer:	D&H Sales
	5549 Denny Ave
	N. Hollywood, CA 91601
	818-762-9191, FAX 818-762-1171
Demo:	http://noad.com/Nsoft.htm
Sound output:	Mac internal, MIDI

Name:	**Tab Transcriber 2.04 - converts MIDI to guitar TAB**
Platforms:	MS-DOS

Requirements:	386, 4 Megs RAM
List price:	$30
Manufacturer:	Michel Brazeau, mibra@cam.org
Demo:	Yes
To acquire:	Contact author

Name:	**WinSong Composer**
Platforms:	MS-Windows
Requirements:	80286 or better running Windows 3.1, 8MB RAM
List price:	$79.95
Manufacturer:	Softronics
	5085 List Dr.
	Colorado Springs, CO 80919
	800-225-8590, 719-593-9540, 719-548-1878 (fax)
Demo:	http://www.softronics. com
Review:	*Electronic Musician* (December 1993)
Sound output:	MIDI

INDEX